MONDEGREENS:
ALMOST REMEMBERED POEMS

A catalogue record for this book is available from the National Library of Australia

NATIONAL LIBRARY OF AUSTRALIA

© Julie Morrigan (Introduction, Note on the Text, Index of Poets, Index of First Lines, Index of Titles)

Published 2021

ISBN: 978-0-6453437-2-4 (epub)
ISBN: 978-0-6453437-3-1 (paperback)
ISBN: 978-0-6453437-4-8 (PDF)

9 780645 343731

Published by Jumble Books and Publishers, Albany, Western Australia.

Mondegreens

Almost remembered poems

edited by

Julie Morrigan

Contents

Introduction

The past is a foreign country; they do things differently there—Leslie Poles Hartley (1895-1972), 1953.

I started my blog, *From Troubles of the World*, in October 2011 on WordPress. I started it twice. The first iteration died almost at once (I have forgotten why) and, when I went back to start it again a few days later, I misremembered the line of the poem being used to name the blog so the URL came out as 'fromtroublesofthisworld.wordpress.com' instead of 'fromtroublesoftheworld.wordpress.com'. This mistake—and my panicked attempts to rectify it— gave rise to my moniker on the blog (and elsewhere) of 'flusteredduck'. The current blog dates from 15 October 2011 so has just had its tenth anniversary. There are no plans for it to end any time soon.

Initially, the blog was set up as a repository of poetry garnered from my reading. I have always had a love of 'old' books and I was regularly frustrated by tags and quotes of poetry in them. These fragments of poetry were usually in the nature of throwaway references— sometimes a character would use a quotation in conversation or there would be mention of a poem being used as emotional solace or inspiration. It always seemed very clear to me that, at the time what I was reading had been written, the poem being referred to had been so well known that the writer had no need to give it any context as the reader would—of course—have the knowledge of the poem and know all its associated nuances. That familiar and probably universal knowledge had, unlike the book

i

itself, not survived to reach me. This made me feel that I was missing part of the story and it drove me a little crazy.

I was reading the *Fairacres* series by Miss Read (aka Dora Saint) in October 2011. The series was (and still is) easy and pleasant reading but it was full of poetic tags. I had managed to overlook most of them as they had enough setting in the story to make sense but had reached a scene where the schoolteacher was comforting the cleric by mentioning a poem she read when she was troubled. Several lines of the poem were quoted and they intrigued me so much that I wondered if I could find the rest of the poem. It was at that point that I realised that, with the rise of search engines and sites devoted to digitising books, I could type in a line of a poem—any poem—and find not only the rest of the poem but its writer and, often, the time when it had either been composed or published. This led to setting up the blog so those poems would be there again the next time I looked.

The poem that started my search and led to the blog was also the poem that gave the blog its title: *Ducks* by Frederick William Harvey. It is the first poem on the blog but cannot be included here or in the rest of this anthology as it is not yet in the public domain. It begins with the line: 'From troubles of the world I turn to ducks'. It is still one of my favourite poems.

A month or so after I began hunting down and posting poems from books I was reading or had read, I decided to try and post a thousand-and-one poems with each poem by a different poet and with a new poem posted daily. I was reading a new version of *The*

Book of The Thousand Nights and One Night (1923) translated into English by Edward Powys Mathers (1892-1939) from the French translation from the Arabic of Joseph Charles Mardrus (1868-1949) which explains why I picked that particular number. The number was passed years ago and now I tell myself I am curious to see how long I can keep the blog running without repeating a poet.

This collection is of public domain poems from the first four months of the blog. As I went through the poems, I realised I often misremembered words, phrases or whole lines. This problem with remembering words is such a common feature, especially in relation to song lyrics, that it has its own term. As the anthology seems to me to be full of almost-remembered poems, it felt apt to name it after misremembering or mishearing words: *Mondegreens*.

Julie Morrigan
November 2021

Note on the Text

For easy reference (and because I am just like that), I have compiled full indices of poets with their biographical dates when known, first lines and titles.

As well as trying to make sure I have attributed the correct writer for each poem, I have tried to give the year in which a poem was written or published and have attempted to be as accurate as possible. There may be mistakes, however, and for those I apologise and, if you find any, please swing by to *From Troubles of the World* and leave a comment.

I have consciously attempted to include whole poems, even if generally only a few lines of a poem became familiar enough at one time to count as common knowledge. I hope you find this as revelatory as I did.

Upon A Child
—Robert Herrick (1591-1674)

Here a pretty baby lies
Sung asleep with Lullabies:
Pray be silent, and not stirre
Th' easie earth that covers her.

Poem 641 in *Hesperides; or The Works Both Human and Divine of Robert Herrick*, first published in 1648.

When Lovely Woman Stoops to Folly
—Oliver Goldsmith (?1728-1774)

When lovely woman stoops to folly,
  And finds too late that men betray,
What charm can sooth her melancholy,
  What art can wash her guilt away?
The only art her guilt to cover,
  To hide her shame from every eye,
To give repentance to her lover,
  And wring his bosom—is to die.

Appeared in *The Vicar of Wakefield*, first published in 1766

From the Shore
—Carl Sandburg (1878-1967)

A lone gray bird,
Dim-dipping, far-flying,
Alone in the shadows and grandeurs and tumults
Of night and the sea
And the stars and storms.

Out over the darkness it wavers and hovers,
Out into the gloom it swings and batters,
Out into the wind and the rain and the vast,
Out into the pit of a great black world,
Where fogs are at battle, sky-driven, sea-blown,
Love of mist and rapture of flight,
Glories of chance and hazards of death
On its eager and palpitant wings.

Out into the deep of the great dark world,
Beyond the long borders where foam and drift
Of the sundering waves are lost and gone
On the tides that plunge and rear and crumble.

Appeared in *Chicago Poems*, first published in 1916.

Futility
—Wilfred Owen (1893-1918)

Move him into the sun—
Gently its touch awoke him once,
At home, whispering of fields unsown.
Always it awoke him, even in France,
Until this morning and this snow.
If anything might rouse him now
The kind old sun will know.
Think how it wakes the seeds—
Woke, once, the clays of a cold star.
Are limbs so dear-achieved, are sides
Full-nerved,—still warm,—too hard to stir?
Was it for this the clay grew tall?
—O what made fatuous sunbeams toil
To break earth's sleep at all?

First published in *The Nation* on 15 June 1918.

4

I Do Not Like Thee, Doctor Fell
—Tom Brown (1662-1704)

I do not like thee, Doctor Fell,
The reason why I cannot tell;
But this I know, and know full well,
I do not like thee, Doctor Fell.

This translation of Martial's 32nd epigram was supposedly done on the spot by Tom Brown when he was caught in mischief by Dr John Fell (Dean of Christ Church College and Bishop of Oxford) while a student at Oxford University in 1680. The story is considered apocryphal but the translation was so popular it became an English nursery rhyme.

From Greenland's Icy Mountains
—Reginald Heber (1783-1826)

From Greenland's icy mountains, from India's coral
strand;
Where Africa's sunny fountains roll down their golden
sand:
From many an ancient river, from many a palmy plain,
They call us to deliver their land from error's chain.

What though the spicy breezes blow soft o'er Ceylon's
isle;
Though every prospect pleases, and only man is vile?
In vain with lavish kindness the gifts of God are
strown;
The heathen in his blindness bows down to wood and
stone.

Shall we, whose souls are lighted with wisdom from
on high,
Shall we to those benighted the lamp of life deny?
Salvation! O salvation! The joyful sound proclaim,
Till earth's remotest nation has learned Messiah's
Name.

Waft, waft, ye winds, His story, and you, ye waters,
roll
Till, like a sea of glory, it spreads from pole to pole:
Till o'er our ransomed nature the Lamb for sinners
slain,
Redeemer, King, Creator, in bliss returns to reign.

First published in *Hymns Written and Adapted to the Weekly Church Service of the Year* which was published in 1827.

I Dreamt That I Dwelt in Marble Halls
—Alfred Bunn (1796-1860)

I dreamt that I dwelt in marble halls,
With vassals and serfs at my side,
And of all who assembled within those walls,
That I was the hope and the pride.

I had riches too great to count, could boast
Of a high ancestral name;
But I also dreamt, which pleased me most,
That you lov'd me still the same...

I dreamt that suitors sought my hand;
That knights upon bended knee,
And with vows no maiden heart could withstand,
They pledg'd their faith to me;

And I dreamt that one of that noble host
Came forth my hand to claim.
But I also dreamt, which charmed me most,
That you lov'd me still the same...

I Dreamt That I Dwelt in Marble Halls (also known as *The Gypsy Girl's Dream*) is an aria from *The Bohemian Girl*, an opera by Michael William Balfe with a libretto by Alfred Bunn, first performed in 1843.

Mulga Bill's Bicycle
—Andrew Barton Paterson (1864-1941)

'Twas Mulga Bill, from Eaglehawk, that caught the
    cycling craze;
He turned away the good old horse that served him
    many days;
He dressed himself in cycling clothes, resplendent to
    be seen;
He hurried off to town and bought a shining new
    machine;
And as he wheeled it through the door, with air of
    lordly pride
The grinning shop assistant said, 'Excuse me, can you
    ride?'

'See here, young man,' said Mulga Bill, 'from Walgett
    to the sea,
From Conroy's Gap to Castlereagh, there's none can
    ride like me.
I'm good all round at everything as everybody knows,
Although I'm not the one to talk – I *hate* a man that
    blows.
But riding is my special gift, my chiefest, sole delight;
Just ask a wild duck can it swim, a wildcat can it fight.
There's nothing clothed in hair or hide, or built of
    flesh or steel,
There's nothing walks or jumps, or runs, on axle, hoof,
    or wheel,
But what I'll sit, while hide will hold and girths and
    straps are tight:
I'll ride this here two-wheeled concern right straight
    away at sight.'

'Twas Mulga Bill, from Eaglehawk, that sought his
    own abode,
That perched above Dead Man's Creek, beside the
    mountain road.
He turned the cycle down the hill and mounted for
    the fray,
But 'ere he'd gone a dozen yards it bolted clean away.
It left the track, and through the trees, just like a silver
    streak,
It whistled down the awful slope towards the Dead
    Man's Creek.

It shaved a stump by half an inch, it dodged a big
    white-box:
The very wallaroos in fright went scrambling up the
    rocks,
The wombats hiding in their caves dug deeper
    underground,
As Mulga Bill, as white as chalk, sat tight to every
    bound.
It struck a stone and gave a spring that cleared a
    fallen tree,
It raced beside a precipice as close as close could be;
And then as Mulga Bill let out one last despairing
    shriek
It made a leap of twenty feet into the Dean Man's
    Creek.

'Twas Mulga Bill, from Eaglehawk, that slowly swam
    ashore:
He said, 'I've had some narrer shaves and lively rides
    before;
I've rode a wild bull round a yard to win a five-pound
    bet,

But this was the most awful ride that I've
    encountered yet.
I'll give that two-wheeled outlaw best; it's shaken all
    my nerve
To feel it whistle through the air and plunge and buck
    and swerve.
It's safe at rest in Dead Man's Creek, we'll leave it
    lying still;
A horse's back is good enough henceforth for Mulga
    Bill.'

First published in *The Sydney Mail* in 1896.

A Study (A Soul)
—Christina Rossetti (1830-1894)

She stands as pale as Parian statues stand;
Like Cleopatra when she turned at bay,
And felt her strength above the Roman sway,
And felt the aspic writhing in her hand.
Her face is steadfast toward the shadowy land,
For dim beyond it looms the light of day;
Her feet are steadfast; all the arduous way
That foot-track hath not wavered on the sand.
She stands there like a beacon thro' the night,
A pale clear beacon where the storm-drift is;
She stands alone, a wonder deathly white;
She stands there patient, nerved with inner might,
Indomitable in her feebleness,
Her face and will athirst against the light.

First published in 1896 in *New Poems: Hitherto Unpublished or Uncollected*, two years after her death, but known to have been written in 1854.

Sonnet 43
—Elizabeth Barrett Browning (1806-1861)

How do I love thee? Let me count the ways.
I love thee to the depth and breadth and height
My soul can reach, when feeling out of sight
For the ends of Being and ideal Grace.
I love thee to the level of every day's
Most quiet need, by sun and candle-light.
I love thee freely, as men strive for Right;
I love thee purely, as they turn from Praise.
I love thee with a passion put to use
In my old griefs, and with my childhood's faith.
I love thee with a love I seemed to lose
With my lost saints, — I love thee with the breath,
Smiles, tears, of all my life! — and, if God choose,
I shall but love thee better after death.

Appeared in *Sonnets from the Portuguese*, first published in
1850 and written between 1845 and 1846.

Halloween
—Robert Burns (1759-1796)

Upon that night, when fairies light
On Cassilis Downans dance,
Or owre the lays, in splendid blaze,
On sprightly coursers prance;
Or for Colean the route is ta'en,
Beneath the moon's pale beams;
There, up the cove, to stray and rove,
Among the rocks and streams
To sport that night.

Among the bonny winding banks,
Where Doon rins, wimplin' clear,
Where Bruce ance ruled the martial ranks,
And shook his Carrick spear,
Some merry, friendly, country-folks,
Together did convene,
To burn their nits, and pou their stocks,
And haud their Halloween
Fu' blithe that night.

The lasses feat, and cleanly neat,
Mair braw than when they're fine;
Their faces blithe, fu' sweetly kythe,
Hearts leal, and warm, and kin';
The lads sae trig, wi' wooer-babs,
Weel knotted on their garten,
Some unco blate, and some wi' gabs,
Gar lasses' hearts gang startin'
Whiles fast at night.

Then, first and foremost, through the kail,
Their stocks maun a' be sought ance;
They steek their een, and graip and wale,
For muckle anes and straught anes.
Poor hav'rel Will fell aff the drift,
And wander'd through the bow-kail,
And pou't, for want o' better shift,
A runt was like a sow-tail,
Sae bow't that night.

Then, staught or crooked, yird or nane,
They roar and cry a' throu'ther;
The very wee things, todlin', rin,
Wi' stocks out owre their shouther;
And gif the custoc's sweet or sour.
Wi' joctelegs they taste them;
Syne cozily, aboon the door,
Wi cannie care, they've placed them
To lie that night.

The lasses staw frae 'mang them a'
To pou their stalks of corn:
But Rab slips out, and jinks about,
Behint the muckle thorn:
He grippet Nelly hard and fast;
Loud skirl'd a' the lasses;
But her tap-pickle maist was lost,
When kitlin' in the fause-house
Wi' him that night.

The auld guidwife's well-hoordit nits,
Are round and round divided,
And monie lads' and lasses' fates
Are there that night decided:
Some kindle coothie, side by side,

And burn thegither trimly;
Some start awa, wi' saucy pride,
And jump out-owre the chimlie
Fu' high that night.

Jean slips in twa wi' tentie ee;
Wha 'twas she wadna tell;
But this is Jock, and this is me,
She says in to hersel:
He bleezed owre her, and she owre him,
As they wad never mair part;
Till, fuff! he started up the lum,
And Jean had e'en a sair heart
To see't that night.

Poor Willie, wi' his bow-kail runt,
Was brunt wi' primsie Mallie;
And Mallie, nae doubt, took the drunt,
To be compared to Willie;
Mall's nit lap out wi' pridefu' fling,
And her ain fit it brunt it;
While Willie lap, and swore by jing,
'Twas just the way he wanted
To be that night.

Nell had the fause-house in her min',
She pits hersel and Rob in;
In loving bleeze they sweetly join,
Till white in ase they're sobbin';
Nell's heart was dancin' at the view,
She whisper'd Rob to leuk for't:
Rob, stowlins, prie'd her bonny mou',
Fu' cozie in the neuk for't,
Unseen that night.

But Merran sat behint their backs,
Her thoughts on Andrew Bell;
She lea'es them gashin' at their cracks,
And slips out by hersel:
She through the yard the nearest taks,
And to the kiln goes then,
And darklins graipit for the bauks,
And in the blue-clue throws then,
Right fear't that night.

And aye she win't, and aye she swat,
I wat she made nae jaukin',
Till something held within the pat,
Guid Lord! but she was quakin'!
But whether 'was the deil himsel,
Or whether 'twas a bauk-en',
Or whether it was Andrew Bell,
She didna wait on talkin'
To spier that night.

Wee Jennie to her grannie says,
'Will ye go wi' me, grannie?
I'll eat the apple at the glass
I gat frae Uncle Johnnie:'
She fuff't her pipe wi' sic a lunt,
In wrath she was sae vap'rin',
She notice't na, an aizle brunt
Her braw new worset apron
Out through that night.

'Ye little skelpie-limmer's face!
I daur you try sic sportin',
As seek the foul thief ony place,
For him to spae your fortune.
Nae doubt but ye may get a sight!

Great cause ye hae to fear it;
For mony a ane has gotten a fright,
And lived and died deleeret
On sic a night.

'Ae hairst afore the Sherramoor, —
I mind't as weel's yestreen,
I was a gilpey then, I'm sure
I wasna past fifteen;
The simmer had been cauld and wat,
And stuff was unco green;
And aye a rantin' kirn we gat,
And just on Halloween
It fell that night.

'Our stibble-rig was Rab M'Graen,
A clever sturdy fallow:
His son gat Eppie Sim wi' wean,
That lived in Achmacalla:
He gat hemp-seed, I mind it weel,
And he made unco light o't;
But mony a day was by himsel,
He was sae sairly frighted
That very night.'

Then up gat fechtin' Jamie Fleck,
And he swore by his conscience,
That he could saw hemp-seed a peck;
For it was a' but nonsense.
The auld guidman raught down the pock,
And out a hanfu' gied him;
Syne bade him slip frae 'mang the folk,
Some time when nae ane see'd him,
And try't that night.

He marches through amang the stacks,
Though he was something sturtin;
The graip he for a harrow taks.
And haurls it at his curpin;
And every now and then he says,
'Hemp-seed, I saw thee,
And her that is to be my lass,
Come after me, and draw thee
As fast this night.'

He whistled up Lord Lennox' march
To keep his courage cheery;
Although his hair began to arch,
He was say fley'd and eerie:
Till presently he hears a squeak,
And then a grane and gruntle;
He by his shouther gae a keek,
And tumbled wi' a wintle
Out-owre that night.

He roar'd a horrid murder-shout,
In dreadfu' desperation!
And young and auld came runnin' out
To hear the sad narration;
He swore 'twas hilchin Jean M'Craw,
Or crouchie Merran Humphie,
Till, stop! she trotted through them
And wha was it but grumphie
Asteer that night!

Meg fain wad to the barn hae gaen,
To win three wechts o' naething;
But for to meet the deil her lane,
She pat but little faith in:
She gies the herd a pickle nits,

And two red-cheekit apples,
To watch, while for the barn she sets,
In hopes to see Tam Kipples
That very nicht.

She turns the key wi cannie thraw,
And owre the threshold ventures;
But first on Sawnie gies a ca'
Syne bauldly in she enters:
A ratton rattled up the wa',
And she cried, Lord, preserve her!
And ran through midden-hole and a',
And pray'd wi' zeal and fervour,
Fu' fast that night;

They hoy't out Will wi' sair advice;
They hecht him some fine braw ane;
It chanced the stack he faddom'd thrice
Was timmer-propt for thrawin';
He taks a swirlie, auld moss-oak,
For some black grousome carlin;
And loot a winze, and drew a stroke,
Till skin in blypes cam haurlin'
Aff's nieves that night.

A wanton widow Leezie was,
As canty as a kittlin;
But, och! that night amang the shaws,
She got a fearfu' settlin'!
She through the whins, and by the cairn,
And owre the hill gaed scrievin,
Whare three lairds' lands met at a burn
To dip her left sark-sleeve in,
Was bent that night.

Whyles owre a linn the burnie plays,
As through the glen it wimpl't;
Whyles round a rocky scaur it strays;
Whyles in a wiel it dimpl't;
Whyles glitter'd to the nightly rays,
Wi' bickering, dancing dazzle;
Whyles cookit underneath the braes,
Below the spreading hazel,
Unseen that night.

Among the brackens, on the brae,
Between her and the moon,
The deil, or else an outler quey,
Gat up and gae a croon:
Poor Leezie's heart maist lap the hool!
Near lav'rock-height she jumpit;
but mist a fit, and in the pool
Out-owre the lugs she plumpit,
Wi' a plunge that night.

In order, on the clean hearth-stane,
The luggies three are ranged,
And every time great care is ta'en',
To see them duly changed:
Auld Uncle John, wha wedlock joys
Sin' Mar's year did desire,
Because he gat the toom dish thrice,
He heaved them on the fire
In wrath that night.

Wi' merry sangs, and friendly cracks,
I wat they didna weary;
And unco tales, and funny jokes,
Their sports were cheap and cheery;
Till butter'd so'ns, wi' fragrant lunt,

Set a' their gabs a-steerin';
Syne, wi' a social glass o' strunt,
They parted aff careerin'
Fu' blythe that night.

First published in 1786 in *Poems, Chiefly in the Scottish Dialect*.

Dinah in Heaven
—Rudyard Kipling (1865-1936)

She did not know that she was dead,
But, when the pang was o'er,
Sat down to wait her Master's tread
Upon the Golden Floor,

With ears full-cock and anxious eye
Impatiently resigned;
But ignorant that Paradise
Did not admit her kind.

Persons with Haloes, Harps, and Wings
Assembled and reproved;
Or talked to her of Heavenly things,
But Dinah never moved.

There was one step along the Stair
That led to Heaven's Gate;
And, till she heard it, her affair
Was—she explained—to wait.

And she explained with flattened ear,
Bared lip and milky tooth—
Storming against Ithuriel's Spear
That only proved her truth!

Sudden—far down the Bridge of Ghosts
That anxious spirits clomb—
She caught that step in all the hosts,
And knew that he had come.

She left them wondering what to do,
But not a doubt had she.
Swifter than her own squeal she flew
Across the Glassy Sea;

Flushing the Cherubs every where,
And skidding as she ran,
She refuged under Peter's Chair
And waited for her man.

. . . .

There spoke a Spirit out of the press,
Said:—'Have you any here
That saved a fool from drunkenness,
And a coward from his fear?

'That turned a soul from dark to day
When other help was vain;
That snatched it from wanhope and made
A cur a man again?'

'Enter and look,' said Peter then,
And set The Gate ajar.
'If I know aught of women and men
I trow she is not far.'

'Neither by virtue, speech nor art
Nor hope of grace to win;
But godless innocence of heart
That never heard of sin:

'Neither by beauty nor belief
Nor white example shown.

Something a wanton—more a thief—
But—most of all—mine own.'

'Enter and look,' said Peter then,
'And send you well to speed;
But, for all that I know of women and men
Your riddle is hard to read.'

Then flew Dinah from under the Chair,
Into his arms she flew—
And licked his face from chin to hair
And Peter passed them through!

First appeared in the short story, *The Woman in his Life*,
from *Limits and Renewals,* published in 1932.

Song of the Witches
—William Shakespeare (1564-1616)

Round about the cauldron go;
In the poison'd entrails throw.
Toad, that under cold stone
Days and nights has thirty-one
Swelter'd venom sleeping got,
Boil thou first i' the charmed pot.

Double, double toil and trouble;
Fire burn and caldron bubble.

Fillet of a fenny snake,
In the cauldron boil and bake;
Eye of newt and toe of frog,
Wool of bat and tongue of dog,
Adder's fork and blind-worm's sting,
Lizard's leg and owlet's wing,
For a charm of powerful trouble,
Like a hell-broth boil and bubble.
Double, double toil and trouble;
Fire burn and caldron bubble.

Scale of dragon, tooth of wolf,
Witches' mummy, maw and gulf
Of the ravin'd salt-sea shark,
Root of hemlock digg'd i' the dark,
Liver of blaspheming Jew,
Gall of goat, and slips of yew
Silver'd in the moon's eclipse,

Nose of Turk and Tartar's lips,
Finger of birth-strangled babe
Ditch-deliver'd by a drab,
Make the gruel thick and slab:
Add thereto a tiger's chaudron,
For the ingredients of our cauldron

Double, double toil and trouble;
Fire burn and cauldron bubble.

Cool it with a baboon's blood,
Then the charm is firm and good.

From *The Tragedy of MacBeth* (also known as *The Scottish Play* and *MacBeth*), first performed around 1606.

In Flanders Fields
—John McCrae (1872-1918)

In Flanders Fields the poppies blow
Between the crosses, row on row,
That mark our place; and in the sky
The larks, still bravely singing, fly
Scarce heard amid the guns below.

We are the dead. Short days ago
We lived, felt dawn, saw sunset glow,
Loved, and were loved, and now we lie
In Flanders Fields.

Take up our quarrel with the foe:
To you from failing hands we throw
The torch; be yours to hold it high.
If ye break faith with us who die
We shall not sleep, though poppies grow
In Flanders Fields.

First published on 8 December 1915 in *Punch*.

Heaven-Haven
—Gerard Manley Hopkins (1844-1899)

A nun takes the veil

I have desired to go
Where springs not fail,
To fields where flies no sharp and sided hail
And a few lilies blow.

And I have asked to be
Where no storms come,
Where the green swell is in the havens dumb,
And out of the swing of the sea.

Written around 1865 but not published until 1918 after the poet's death.

When the Frost is on the Punkin
—James Whitcomb Riley (1853-1916)

When the frost is on the punkin and the fodder's in
    the shock,
And you hear the kyouck and gobble of the struttin'
    turkey-cock,
And the clackin' of the guineys, and the cluckin' of the
    hens,
And the rooster's hallylooyer as he tiptoes on the
    fence;
O, it's then the time a feller is a-feelin' at his best,
With the risin' sun to greet him from a night of
    peaceful rest,
As he leaves the house, bareheaded, and goes out to
    feed the stock,
When the frost is on the punkin and the fodder's in
    the shock.

They's something kindo' harty-like about the
    atmusfere
When the heat of summer's over and the coolin' fall is
    here—
Of course we miss the flowers, and the blossoms on
    the trees,
And the mumble of the hummin'-birds and buzzin' of
    the bees;
But the air's so appetizin'; and the landscape through
    the haze
Of a crisp and sunny morning of the airly autumn days
Is a pictur' that no painter has the colorin' to mock—
When the frost is on the punkin and the fodder's in
    the shock.

The husky, rusty russel of the tossels of the corn,
And the raspin' of the tangled leaves as golden as the
morn;
The stubble in the furries—kindo' lonesome-like, but
still
A-preachin' sermuns to us of the barns they growed
to fill;
The strawstack in the medder, and the reaper in the
shed;
The hosses in theyr stalls below—the clover
overhead!—
O, it sets my hart a-clickin' like the tickin' of a clock,
When the frost is on the punkin and the fodder's in
the shock.

Then your apples all is gethered, and the ones a feller
keeps
Is poured around the cellar-floor in red and yaller
heaps;
And your cider-makin's over, and your wimmern-folks
is through
With theyr mince and apple-butter, and theyr souse
and sausage too!...
don't know how to tell it—but ef such a thing could
be
As the angels wantin' boardin', and they'd call around
on *me*—
I'd want to 'commodate 'em—all the whole-indurin'
flock—
When the frost is on the punkin and the fodder's in
the shock.

Appeared in *The old swimmin'-hole" and 'leven more poems.: Neghborly [!] poems on friendship, grief and farm-life*, first published in 1883.

Song
—John Donne (1572-1631)

Go and catch a falling star,
Get with child a mandrake root,
Tell me where all past years are,
Or who cleft the devil's foot,
Teach me to hear mermaids singing,
Or to keep off envy's stinging,
And find
What wind
Serves to advance an honest mind.

If thou be'st born to strange sights,
Things invisible to see,
Ride ten thousand days and nights,
Till age snow white hairs on thee,
Thou, when thou return'st, wilt tell me,
All strange wonders that befell thee,
And swear,
No where
Lives a woman true and fair.

If thou find'st one, let me know,
Such a pilgrimage were sweet;
Yet do not, I would not go,
Though at next door we might meet,
Though she were true, when you met her,
And last, till you write your letter,
Yet she
Will be
False, ere I come, to two, or three.

First published in 1633 after John Donne's death but probably written at some time in the 1590s.

Crossing the Bar
—Alfred Tennyson (1809-1892)

Sunset and evening star,
  And one clear call for me!
And may there be no moaning of the bar,
  When I put out to sea,

But such a tide as moving seems asleep,
  Too full for sound and foam,
When that which drew from out the boundless deep
  Turns again home.

Twilight and evening bell,
And after that the dark!
And may there be no sadness of farewell,
  When I embark;

For tho' from out our bourne of Time and Place
  The flood may bear me far,
I hope to see my Pilot face to face
  When I have crost the bar.

Written in 1889 and, by Tennyson's own request, usually
the last poem in all editions of his poems.

The Passionate Shepherd to His Love
—Christopher Marlowe (1564-1593)

Come live with me and be my Love,
And we will all the pleasures prove
That hills and valleys, dale and field,
And all the craggy mountains yield.

There will we sit upon the rocks
And see the shepherds feed their flocks,
By shallow rivers, to whose falls
Melodious birds sing madrigals.

There will I make thee beds of roses
And a thousand fragrant posies,
A cap of flowers, and a kirtle
Embroider'd all with leaves of myrtle.

A gown made of the finest wool
Which from our pretty lambs we pull,
Fair linèd slippers for the cold,
With buckles of the purest gold.

A belt of straw and ivy buds
With coral clasps and amber studs:
And if these pleasures may thee move,
Come live with me and be my Love.

Thy silver dishes for thy meat
As precious as the gods do eat,
Shall on an ivory table be
Prepared each day for thee and me.

The shepherd swains shall dance and sing
For thy delight each May-morning:
If these delights thy mind may move,
Then live with me and be my Love.

First published in 1599, six years after his death.

Dover Beach
—Matthew Arnold (1822-1888)

The sea is calm to-night.
The tide is full, the moon lies fair
Upon the straits; on the French coast the light
Gleams and is gone; the cliffs of England stand;
Glimmering and vast, out in the tranquil bay.
Come to the window, sweet is the night-air!
Only, from the long line of spray
Where the sea meets the moon-blanched land,
Listen! you hear the grating roar
Of pebbles which the waves draw back, and fling,
At their return, up the high strand,
Begin, and cease, and then again begin,
With tremulous cadence slow, and bring
The eternal note of sadness in.

Sophocles long ago
Heard it on the Ægaean, and it brought
Into his mind the turbid ebb and flow
Of human misery; we
Find also in the sound a thought,
Hearing it by this distant northern sea.

The Sea of Faith
Was once, too, at the full, and round earth's shore
Lay like the folds of a bright girdle furled.
But now I only hear
Its melancholy, long, withdrawing roar,
Retreating, to the breath
Of the night-wind, down the vast edges drear
And naked shingles of the world.

Ah, love, let us be true
To one another! for the world, which seems
To lie before us like a land of dreams,
So various, so beautiful, so new,
Hath really neither joy, nor love, nor light,
Nor certitude, nor peace, nor help for pain;
And we are here as on a darkling plain
Swept with confused alarms of struggle and flight,
Where ignorant armies clash by night.

Appeared in *New Poems*, first published in 1867, but
thought to have been written around 1851.

A Song of Sherwood
—Alfred Noyes (1880-1958)

Sherwood in the twilight, is Robin Hood awake?
Grey and ghostly shadows are gliding through the
    brake,
Shadows of the dappled deer, dreaming of the morn,
Dreaming of a shadowy man that winds a shadowy
    horn.

Robin Hood is here again: all his merry thieves
Hear a ghostly bugle-note shivering through the
    leaves,
Calling as he used to call, faint and far away,
In Sherwood, in Sherwood, about the break of day.

Merry, merry England has kissed the lips of June:
All the wings of fairyland were here beneath the
    moon,
Like a flight of rose-leaves fluttering in a mist
Of opal and ruby and pearl and amethyst.

Merry, merry England is waking as of old,
With eyes of blither hazel and hair of brighter gold:
For Robin Hood is here again beneath the bursting
    spray
In Sherwood, in Sherwood, about the break of day.

Love is in the greenwood building him a house
Of wild rose and hawthorn and honeysuckle boughs:
Love is in the greenwood, dawn is in the skies,
And Marian is waiting with a glory in her eyes.

Hark! The dazzled laverock climbs the golden steep!
Marian is waiting: is Robin Hood asleep?
Round the fairy grass-rings frolic elf and fay,
In Sherwood, in Sherwood, about the break of day.

Oberon, Oberon, rake away the gold,
Rake away the red leaves, roll away the mould,
Rake away the gold leaves, roll away the red,
And wake Will Scarlett from his leafy forest bed.

Friar Tuck and Little John are riding down together
With quarter-staff and drinking-can and grey goose-
    feather.
The dead are coming back again, the years are rolled
    away
In Sherwood, in Sherwood, about the break of day.

Softly over Sherwood the south wind blows.
All the heart of England his in every rose
Hears across the greenwood the sunny whisper leap,
Sherwood in the red dawn, is Robin Hood asleep?

Hark, the voice of England wakes him as of old
And, shattering the silence with a cry of brighter gold
Bugles in the greenwood echo from the steep,
Sherwood in the red dawn, is Robin Hood asleep?

Where the deer are gliding down the shadowy glen
All across the glades of fern he calls his merry men—
Doublets of the Lincoln green glancing through the
    May
In Sherwood, in Sherwood, about the break of day—

Calls them and they answer: from aisles of oak and
    ash
Rings the Follow! Follow! and the boughs begin to
    crash,
The ferns begin to flutter and the flowers begin to fly,
And through the crimson dawning the robber band
    goes by.

Robin! Robin! Robin! All his merry thieves
Answer as the bugle-note shivers through the leaves,
Calling as he used to call, faint and far away,
In Sherwood, in Sherwood, about the break of day.

First published as 'Sherwood' in *The Literary Digest*,
Volume 27, on 5 December 1903.

Coventry Carol
—Robert Croo (fl. 1534)

Lully, lullay, thou little tiny child,
bye, bye, lully lullay.

O sisters too, how may we do,
for to preserve this day,
this poor youngling for whom we sing,
bye, bye lully lullay.

Herod the king in his raging,
charged he hath this day,
his men of night, in his own sight,
all young children to slay.

Then woe is me, poor child, for thee!
And every morn and day,
for thy parting not say nor sing
bye, bye, lully lullay.

Lully, lullay, thou little tiny child,
bye, bye, lully lullay.

Traditional English carol performed in a mystery play (*The Pageant of the Shearmen and Tailors*), written down in this form by Robert Croo in 1534.

The Children's Hour
—Henry Wadsworth Longfellow (1807-1882)

Between the dark and the daylight,
 When the night is beginning to lower,
Comes a pause in the day's occupations,
 That is known as the Children's Hour.

I hear in the chamber above me
 The patter of little feet,
The sound of a door that is opened,
 And voices soft and sweet.

From my study I see in the lamplight,
 Descending the broad hall stair,
Grave Alice, and laughing Allegra,
 And Edith with golden hair.

A whisper, and then a silence:
 Yet I know by their merry eyes
They are plotting and planning together
 To take me by surprise.

A sudden rush from the stairway,
 A sudden raid from the hall!
By three doors left unguarded
 They enter my castle wall!

They climb up into my turret
 O'er the arms and back of my chair;
If I try to escape, they surround me;
 They seem to be everywhere.

They almost devour me with kisses,
  Their arms about me entwine,
Till I think of the Bishop of Bingen
  In his Mouse-Tower on the Rhine!

Do you think, O blue-eyed banditti,
  Because you have scaled the wall,
Such an old mustache as I am
  Is not a match for you all!

I have you fast in my fortress,
  And will not let you depart,
But put you down into the dungeon
  In the round-tower of my heart.

And there will I keep you forever,
  Yes, forever and a day,
Till the walls shall crumble to ruin,
  And moulder in dust away.

Appeared in *The Atlantic Monthly: A Magazine of Literature, Art, and Politics* in September 1860.

Young Lochinvar
—Walter Scott (1771-1832)

O young Lochinvar is come out of the west,
Through all the wide Border his steed was the best;
And save his good broadsword he weapons had none,
He rode all unarm'd, and he rode all alone.
So faithful in love, and so dauntless in war,
There never was knight like the young Lochinvar.

He staid not for brake, and he stopp'd not for stone,
He swam the Eske river where ford there was none;
But ere he alighted at Netherby gate,
The bride had consented, the gallant came late:
For a laggard in love, and a dastard in war,
Was to wed the fair Ellen of brave Lochinvar.

So boldly he enter'd the Netherby Hall,
Among bride's-men, and kinsmen, and brothers and
    all:
Then spoke the bride's father, his hand on his sword,
(For the poor craven bridegroom said never a word,)
'O come ye in peace here, or come ye in war,
Or to dance at our bridal, young Lord Lochinvar?'

'I long woo'd your daughter, my suit you denied; —
Love swells like the Solway, but ebbs like its tide —
And now I am come, with this lost love of mine,
To lead but one measure, drink one cup of wine.
There are maidens in Scotland more lovely by far,
That would gladly be bride to the young Lochinvar.'

The bride kiss'd the goblet: the knight took it up,
He quaff'd off the wine, and he threw down the cup.

She look'd down to blush, and she look'd up to sigh,
With a smile on her lips and a tear in her eye.
He took her soft hand, ere her mother could bar, —
'Now tread we a measure!' said young Lochinvar.

So stately his form, and so lovely her face,
That never a hall such a gailiard did grace;
While her mother did fret, and her father did fume
And the bridegroom stood dangling his bonnet and
     plume;
And the bride-maidens whisper'd, ' 'twere better by
     far
To have match'd our fair cousin with young
     Lochinvar.'

One touch to her hand, and one word in her ear,
When they reach'd the hall-door, and the charger
     stood near;
So light to the croupe the fair lady he swung,
So light to the saddle before her he sprung!
'She is won! we are gone, over bank, bush, and scaur;
They'll have fleet steeds that follow,' quoth young
     Lochinvar.

There was mounting 'mong Graemes of the Netherby
     clan;
Forsters, Fenwicks, and Musgraves, they rode and
     they ran:
There was racing and chasing on Cannobie Lee,
But the lost bride of Netherby ne'er did they see.
So daring in love, and so dauntless in war,
Have ye e'er heard of gallant like young Lochinvar?

Number XII in Canto Fifth in *Marmion: A Tale of Flodden Field*, first published in 1808.

To His Coy Mistress
—Andrew Marvell (1621-1672)

Had we but world enough, and time,
This coyness, lady, were no crime.
We would sit down and think which way
To walk, and pass our long love's day;
Thou by the Indian Ganges' side
Shouldst rubies find; I by the tide
Of Humber would complain. I would
Love you ten years before the Flood;
And you should, if you please, refuse
Till the conversion of the Jews.
My vegetable love should grow
Vaster than empires, and more slow.
An hundred years should go to praise
Thine eyes, and on thy forehead gaze;
Two hundred to adore each breast,
But thirty thousand to the rest;
An age at least to every part,
And the last age should show your heart.
For, lady, you deserve this state,
Nor would I love at lower rate.

But at my back I always hear
Time's winged chariot hurrying near;
And yonder all before us lie
Deserts of vast eternity.
Thy beauty shall no more be found,
Nor, in thy marble vault, shall sound
My echoing song; then worms shall try
That long preserv'd virginity,
And your quaint honour turn to dust,
And into ashes all my lust.

The grave's a fine and private place,
But none I think do there embrace.

   Now therefore, while the youthful hue
Sits on thy skin like morning dew,
And while thy willing soul transpires
At every pore with instant fires,
Now let us sport us while we may;
And now, like am'rous birds of prey,
Rather at once our time devour,
Than languish in his slow-chapp'd power.
Let us roll all our strength, and all
Our sweetness, up into one ball;
And tear our pleasures with rough strife
Thorough the iron gates of life.
Thus, though we cannot make our sun
Stand still, yet we will make him run.

Published in 1681 after Andrew Marvell's death and
thought to have been written in the 1650s.

Christmas is Coming
—Traditional

Christmas is coming, the goose is getting fat
Please put a penny in the old man's hat
If you haven't got a penny, a ha' penny will do,
If you haven't got a ha' penny, then God bless you!

Traditional English nursery rhyme and Christmas carol,
listed as 12817 in the *Roud Folk Song Index*. It is
traditionally sung to *Country Gardens*, an old English folk
tune, which can be dated back to the early eighteenth
century.

I Wandered Lonely as A Cloud
—William Wordsworth (1770-1850)

I wandered lonely as a cloud
That floats on high o'er vales and hills,
When all at once I saw a crowd,
A host, of golden daffodils;
Beside the lake, beneath the trees,
Fluttering and dancing in the breeze.

Continuous as the stars that shine
And twinkle on the milky way,
They stretched in never-ending line
Along the margin of a bay:
Ten thousand saw I at a glance,
Tossing their heads in sprightly dance.

The waves beside them danced; but they
Out-did the sparkling waves in glee:
A poet could not but be gay,
In such a jocund company:
I gazed—and gazed—but little thought
What wealth the show to me had brought:

For oft, when on my couch I lie
In vacant or in pensive mood,
They flash upon that inward eye
Which is the bliss of solitude;
And then my heart with pleasure fills,
And dances with the daffodils.

Also known as *Daffodils*.

A version of this poem first appeared in Volume I of *Poems, in Two Volumes*, published in 1807, and there is a manuscript version of it from 1802. Wordsworth revised the poem to the current version in 1815.

Life is but a Dream
—Charles Dodgson (Lewis Carroll) (1832-1898)

A boat, beneath a sunny sky
Lingering onward dreamily
In an evening of July

Children three that nestle near,
Eager eye and willing ear,
Pleased a simple tale to hear

Long has paled that sunny sky;
Echoes fade and memories die;
Autumn frosts have slain July.

Still she haunts me, phantomwise,
Alice moving under skies
Never seen by waking eyes.

Children yet, the tale to hear,
Eager eye and willing ear,
Lovingly shall nestle near.

In a Wonderland they lie,
Dreaming as the days go by,
Dreaming as the summers die;

Ever drifting down the stream
Lingering in the golden gleam
Life, what is it but a dream?

Postlude in *Through the Looking-Glass, and What Alice Found There*, published in 1871. It is an acrostic and spells out 'Alice Pleasance Liddell', Alice's full name.

Casabianca
—Felicia Hemans (1793-1835)

The boy stood on the burning deck
  Whence all but he had fled;
The flame that lit the battle's wreck
  Shone round him o'er the dead.

Yet beautiful and bright he stood,
  As born to rule the storm;
A creature of heroic blood,
  A proud, though child-like form.

The flames rolled on—he would not go
  Without his Father's word;
That father, faint in death below,
  His voice no longer heard.

He called aloud—'say, Father, say
  If yet my task is done?'
He knew not that the chieftain lay
  Unconscious of his son.

'Speak, father!' once again he cried,
  'If I may yet be gone!'
And but the booming shots replied,
  And fast the flames rolled on.

Upon his brow he felt their breath,
  And in his waving hair,
And looked from that lone post of death
  In still yet brave despair.

And shouted but once more aloud,
 'My father! must I stay?'
While o'er him fast, through sail and shroud,
 The wreathing fires made way.

They wrapt the ship in splendour wild,
 They caught the flag on high,
And streamed above the gallant child,
 Like banners in the sky.

There came a burst of thunder sound—
 The boy—oh! where was he?
Ask of the winds that far around
 With fragments strewed the sea!—

With mast, and helm, and pennon fair,
 That well had borne their part—
But the noblest thing which perished there
 Was that young faithful heart.

*Young Casabianca, a boy about thirteen years old,
son to the Admiral of the Orient, remained at his post
(in the Battle of the Nile) after the ship had taken fire,
and all the guns had been abandoned, and perished in
the explosion of the vessel, when the flames had
reached the powder.

Appeared in The Monthly Magazine, Volume 2, August
1826.

Song—To Celia
—Ben Jonson (1572-1637)

Drink to me only with thine eyes,
And I will pledge with mine;
Or leave a kiss within the cup,
And I'll not ask for wine
The thirst that from the soul doth rise,
Doth crave a drink divine;
But might I of Jove's nectar sup,
I would not change for thine.

I sent thee late a rosy wreath
Not so much honoring thee
As giving it a hope that there
It could not withered be;
But thou thereon didst only breathe
And sent'st back to me,
Since when it grows and smells, I swear,
Not of itself, but thee.

Number IX in *The Forest*, published in 1616.

The Lady's Dressing Room
—Jonathan Swift (1667-1745)

Five hours, (and who can do it less in?)
By haughty Celia spent in dressing;
The goddess from her chamber issues,
Arrayed in lace, brocades, and tissues.

Strephon, who found the room was void
And Betty otherwise employed,
Stole in and took a strict survey
Of all the litter as it lay;
Whereof, to make the matter clear,
An inventory follows here.

And first a dirty smock appeared,
Beneath the arm-pits well besmeared.
Strephon, the rogue, displayed it wide
And turned it round on every side.
On such a point few words are best,
And Strephon bids us guess the rest;
And swears how damnably the men lie
In calling Celia sweet and cleanly.

Now listen while he next produces
The various combs for various uses,
Filled up with dirt so closely fixt,
No brush could force a way betwixt.

A paste of composition rare,
Sweat, dandruff, powder, lead and hair;
A forehead cloth with oil upon't
To smooth the wrinkles on her front.

Here alum flower to stop the steams
Exhaled from sour unsavory streams;
There night-gloves made of Tripsy's hide,
Bequeath'd by Tripsy when she died,
With puppy water, beauty's help,
Distilled from Tripsy's darling whelp;
Here gallypots and vials placed,
Some filled with washes, some with paste,
Some with pomatum, paints and slops,
And ointments good for scabby chops.

Hard by a filthy basin stands,
Fouled with the scouring of her hands;
The basin takes whatever comes,
The scrapings of her teeth and gums,
A nasty compound of all hues,
For here she spits, and here she spews.

But oh! it turned poor Strephon's bowels,
When he beheld and smelt the towels,
Begummed, besmattered, and beslimed
With dirt, and sweat, and ear-wax grimed.

No object Strephon's eye escapes:
Here petticoats in frowzy heaps;
Nor be the handkerchiefs forgot
All varnished o'er with snuff and snot.

The stockings, why should I expose,
Stained with the marks of stinking toes;
Or greasy coifs and pinners reeking,
Which Celia slept at least a week in?

A pair of tweezers next he found
To pluck her brows in arches round,

Or hairs that sink the forehead low,
Or on her chin like bristles grow.

The virtues we must not let pass,
Of Celia's magnifying glass.
When frighted Strephon cast his eye on't
It shewed the visage of a giant.
A glass that can to sight disclose
The smallest worm in Celia's nose,
And faithfully direct her nail
To squeeze it out from head to tail;
(For catch it nicely by the head,
It must come out alive or dead.)

Why Strephon will you tell the rest?
And must you needs describe the chest?
That careless wench! no creature warn her
To move it out from yonder corner;
But leave it standing full in sight
For you to exercise your spite.

In vain, the workman shewed his wit
With rings and hinges counterfeit
To make it seem in this disguise
A cabinet to vulgar eyes;
For Strephon ventured to look in,
Resolved to go through thick and thin;
He lifts the lid, there needs no more:
He smelt it all the time before.

As from within Pandora's box,
When Epimetheus oped the locks,
A sudden universal crew
Of humane evils upwards flew,
He still was comforted to find

That Hope at last remained behind;
So Strephon lifting up the lid
To view what in the chest was hid,
The vapours flew from out the vent.
But Strephon cautious never meant
The bottom of the pan to grope
And foul his hands in search of Hope.

O never may such vile machine
Be once in Celia's chamber seen!
O may she better learn to keep
'Those secrets of the hoary deep'!
As mutton cutlets, prime of meat,
Which, though with art you salt and beat
As laws of cookery require
And toast them at the clearest fire,
If from adown the hopeful chops
The fat upon the cinder drops,
To stinking smoke it turns the flame
Poisoning the flesh from whence it came;
And up exhales a greasy stench
For which you curse the careless wench;
So things which must not be exprest,
When plumpt into the reeking chest,
Send up an excremental smell
To taint the parts from whence they fell,
The petticoats and gown perfume,
Which waft a stink round every room.

Thus finishing his grand survey,
Disgusted Strephon stole away
Repeating in his amorous fits,
Oh! Celia, Celia, Celia shits!
But vengeance, Goddess never sleeping,
Soon punished Strephon for his peeping:

His foul Imagination links
Each dame he see with all her stinks;
And, if unsavory odors fly,
Conceives a lady standing by.
All women his description fits,
And both ideas jump like wits
By vicious fancy coupled fast,
And still appearing in contrast.

I pity wretched Strephon blind
To all the charms of female kind.
Should I the Queen of Love refuse
Because she rose from stinking ooze?
To him that looks behind the scene
Satira's but some pocky queen.

When Celia in her glory shows,
If Strephon would but stop his nose
(Who now so impiously blasphemes
Her ointments, daubs, and paints and creams,
Her washes, slops, and every clout
With which he makes so foul a rout),
He soon would learn to think like me
And bless his ravished sight to see
Such order from confusion sprung,
Such gaudy tulips raised from dung.

First published in 1732.

Why So Pale and Wan?
—John Suckling (1609-1642)

Why so pale and wan, fond lover?
Prithee, why so pale?
Will, when looking well can't move her,
Looking ill prevail?
Prithee, why so pale?

Why so dull and mute, young sinner?
Prithee, why so mute?
Will, when speaking well can't win her,
Saying nothing do 't?
Prithee, why so mute?

Quit, quit for shame! This will not move;
This cannot take her.
If of herself she will not love,
Nothing can make her:
The devil take her!

Appeared in the play *Aglaura* which was first performed in
1637 and printed in 1638.

Faces in the Street
—Henry Lawson (1867-1922)

They lie, the men who tell us in a loud decisive tone
That want is here a stranger, and that misery's
    unknown;
For where the nearest suburb and the city proper
    meet
My window-sill is level with the faces in the street—
Drifting past, drifting past,
To the beat of weary feet—
While I sorrow for the owners of those faces in the
    street.

And cause I have to sorrow, in a land so young and
    fair,
To see upon those faces stamped the marks of Want
    and Care;
I look in vain for traces of the fresh and fair and sweet
In sallow, sunken faces that are drifting through the
    street—
Drifting on, drifting on,
To the scrape of restless feet;
I can sorrow for the owners of the faces in the street.

In hours before the dawning dims the starlight in the
    sky
The wan and weary faces first begin to trickle by,
Increasing as the moments hurry on with morning
    feet,
Till like a pallid river flow the faces in the street—
Flowing in, flowing in,

To the beat of hurried feet—
Ah! I sorrow for the owners of those faces in the
     street.

The human river dwindles when 'Tis past the hour of
     eight,
Its waves go flowing faster in the fear of being late;
But slowly drag the moments, whilst beneath the dust
     and heat
The city grinds the owners of the faces in the street—
Grinding body, grinding soul,
Yielding scarce enough to eat—
Oh! I sorrow for the owners of the faces in the street.

And then the only faces till the sun is sinking down
Are those of outside toilers and the idlers of the town,
Save here and there a face that seems a stranger in
     the street,
Tells of the city's unemployed upon his weary beat—
Drifting round, drifting round,
To the tread of listless feet—
Ah! My heart aches for the owner of that sad face in
     the street.

And when the hours on lagging feet have slowly
     dragged away,
And sickly yellow gaslights rise to mock the going day,
Then flowing past my window like a tide in its retreat,
Again I see the pallid stream of faces in the street—
Ebbing out, ebbing out,
To the drag of tired feet,
While my heart is aching dumbly for the faces in the
     street.

And now all blurred and smirched with vice the day's
    sad pages end,
For while the short 'large hours' toward the longer
    'small hours' trend,
With smiles that mock the wearer, and with words
    that half entreat,
Delilah pleads for custom at the corner of the street—
Sinking down, sinking down,
Battered wreck by tempests beat—
A dreadful, thankless trade is hers, that Woman of the
    Street.

But, ah! to dreader things than these our fair young
    city comes,
For in its heart are growing thick the filthy dens and
    slums,
Where human forms shall rot away in sties for swine
    unmeet,
And ghostly faces shall be seen unfit for any street—
Rotting out, rotting out,
For the lack of air and meat—
In dens of vice and horror that are hidden from the
    street.

I wonder would the apathy of wealthy men endure
Were all their windows level with the faces of the
    Poor?
Ah! Mammon's slaves, your knees shall knock, your
    hearts in terror beat,
When God demands a reason for the sorrows of the
    street,
The wrong things and the bad things
And the sad things that we meet
In the filthy lane and alley, and the cruel, heartless
    street.

I left the dreadful corner where the steps are never
    still,
And sought another window overlooking gorge and
    hill;
But when the night came dreary with the driving rain
    and sleet,
They haunted me—the shadows of those faces in the
    street,
Flitting by, flitting by,
Flitting by with noiseless feet,
And with cheeks but little paler than the real ones in
    the street.

Once I cried: 'Oh, God Almighty! if Thy might doth still
    endure,
Now show me in a vision for the wrongs of Earth a
    cure.'
And, lo! with shops all shuttered I beheld a city's
    street,
And in the warning distance heard the tramp of many
    feet,
Coming near, coming near,
To a drum's dull distant beat,
And soon I saw the army that was marching down the
    street.

Then, like a swollen river that has broken bank and
    wall,
The human flood came pouring with the red flags
    over all,
And kindled eyes all blazing bright with revolution's
    heat,
And flashing swords reflecting rigid faces in the street.
Pouring on, pouring on,

To a drum's loud threatening beat,
And the war-hymns and the cheering of the people in
the street.

And so it must be while the world goes rolling round
its course,
The warning pen shall write in vain, the warning voice
grow hoarse,
But not until a city feels Red Revolution's feet
Shall its sad people miss awhile the terrors of the
street—
The dreadful everlasting strife
For scarcely clothes and meat
In that pent track of living death—the city's cruel
street.

Appeared in *In the Days When the World Was Wide*, 1896,
and first published in July 1888.

Ode on the Death of A Favourite Cat, Drowned in A Tub of Gold Fishes
—Thomas Gray (1716-1771)

'Twas on a lofty vase's side,
Where China's gayest art had dyed
    The azure flowers that blow;
Demurest of the tabby kind,
The pensive Selima, reclined,
    Gazed on the lake below.

Her conscious tail her joy declared;
The fair round face, the snowy beard,
    The velvet of her paws,
Her coat, that with the tortoise vies,
Her ears of jet, and emerald eyes,
    She saw: and purred applause.

Still had she gazed; but 'midst the tide
Two angel forms were seen to glide,
    The Genii of the stream;
Their scaly armour's Tyrian hue
Thro' richest purple to the view
    Betrayed a golden gleam.

The hapless nymph with wonder saw:
A whisker first and then a claw,
    With many an ardent wish,
She stretched in vain to reach the prize.
What female heart can gold despise?
    What cat's averse to fish?

Presumptuous maid! with looks intent
Again she stretched, again she bent,

Nor knew the gulf between.
(Malignant Fate sat by, and smiled)
The slippery verge her feet beguiled,
   She tumbled headlong in.

Eight times emerging from the flood
She mewed to every watery god,
   Some speedy aid to send.
No Dolphin came, no Nereid stirred;
Nor cruel Tom, nor Susan heard.
   A favourite has no friend!

From hence, ye beauties, undeceived,
Know, one false step is ne'er retrieved,
   And be with caution bold.
Not all that tempts your wandering eyes
And heedless hearts is lawful prize,
   Nor all, that glisters, gold.

Written in 1747 and published in 1748.

1914 V: The Soldier
—Rupert Brooke (1887-1915)

If I should die, think only this of me:
That there's some corner of a foreign field
That is for ever England. There shall be
In that rich earth a richer dust concealed;
A dust whom England bore, shaped, made aware,
Gave, once, her flowers to love, her ways to roam,
A body of England's, breathing English air,
Washed by the rivers, blest by suns of home.

And think, this heart, all evil shed away,
A pulse in the eternal mind, no less
Gives somewhere back the thoughts by England
        given;
Her sights and sounds; dreams happy as her day;
And laughter, learnt of friends; and gentleness,
In hearts at peace, under an English heaven.

Fifth poem of '1914' and first published in *1914 and Other Poems,* 1915.

The Passionate Man's Pilgrimage
—Walter Ralegh (c1552-1618)

[Supposed to be written by one at the point of death]

Give me my scallop-shell of quiet,
   My staff of faith to walk upon,
My scrip of joy, immortal diet,
   My bottle of salvation,
My gown of glory, hope's true gage;
And thus I'll take my pilgrimage.

Blood must be my body's balmer,
   No other balm will there be given;
Whilst my soul, like a quiet palmer,
   Travelleth towards the land of heaven;
Over the silver mountains,
Where spring the nectar fountains :
     There will I kiss
     The bowl of bliss;
And drink mine everlasting fill
Upon every milken hill:
My soul will be a-dry before;
But after, it will thirst no more.
Then by that happy blestful day,
   More peaceful pilgrims I shall see,
That have cast off their rags of clay,
   And walk apparelled fresh like me.
     I'll take them first
     To quench their thirst,
And taste of nectar suckets,
     At those clear wells
     Where sweetness dwells
Drawn up by saints in crystal buckets.

And when our bottles and all we
Are filled with immortality,
Then the blessed paths we'll travel,
Strowed with rubies thick as gravel;
Ceilings of diamonds, sapphire floors,
High walls of coral, and pearly bowers.
From thence to heavens's bribeless hall,
Where no corrupted voices brawl;
No conscience molten into gold,
No forged accuser bought or sold,
No cause deferred, nor vain-spent journey;
For there Christ is the King's Attorney,
Who pleads for all without degrees,
And he hath angels, but no fees.
And when the grand twelve-million jury
Of our sins, with direful fury,
'Gainst our souls black verdicts give,
Christ pleads his death, and then we live.

Be thou my speaker, taintless pleader,
Unblotted lawyer, true proceeder!
Thou giv'st salvation even for alms;
Not with a bribèd lawyer's palms.
And this is my eternal plea
To him that made heaven, earth, and sea,
That, since my flesh must die so soon,
And want a head to dine next noon,
Just at the stroke, when my veins start and spread,
Set on my soul an everlasting head.
Then am I ready, like a palmer fit;
To tread those blest paths which before I writ.

Appeared as an addendum to *Daiphantus* by Anthony Scoloker, published in 1604. It has long been attributed to Walter Ralegh and was supposed to have been written when he was in the Tower of London, facing execution, in 1603.

Auguries of Innocence
—William Blake (1757-1827)

To see a world in a grain of sand,
And a heaven in a wild flower,
Hold infinity in the palm of your hand,
And eternity in an hour.

A robin redbreast in a cage
Puts all heaven in a rage.

A dove-house fill'd with doves and pigeons
Shudders hell thro' all its regions.
A dog starv'd at his master's gate
Predicts the ruin of the state.

A horse misused upon the road
Calls to heaven for human blood.
Each outcry of the hunted hare
A fibre from the brain does tear.

A skylark wounded in the wing,
A cherubim does cease to sing.
The game-cock clipt and arm'd for fight
Does the rising sun affright.

Every wolf's and lion's howl
Raises from hell a human soul.

The wild deer, wand'ring here and there,
Keeps the human soul from care.
The lamb misus'd breeds public strife,
And yet forgives the butcher's knife.

The bat that flits at close of eve
Has left the brain that won't believe.
The owl that calls upon the night
Speaks the unbeliever's fright.

He who shall hurt the little wren
Shall never be belov'd by men.
He who the ox to wrath has mov'd
Shall never be by woman lov'd.

The wanton boy that kills the fly
Shall feel the spider's enmity.
He who torments the chafer's sprite
Weaves a bower in endless night.

The caterpillar on the leaf
Repeats to thee thy mother's grief.
Kill not the moth nor butterfly,
For the last judgement draweth nigh.

He who shall train the horse to war
Shall never pass the polar bar.
The beggar's dog and widow's cat,
Feed them and thou wilt grow fat.

The gnat that sings his summer's song
Poison gets from slander's tongue.
The poison of the snake and newt
Is the sweat of envy's foot.

The poison of the honey bee
Is the artist's jealousy.

The prince's robes and beggar's rags
Are toadstools on the miser's bags.

A truth that's told with bad intent
Beats all the lies you can invent.

It is right it should be so;
Man was made for joy and woe;
And when this we rightly know,
Thro' the world we safely go.

Joy and woe are woven fine,
A clothing for the soul divine.
Under every grief and pine
Runs a joy with silken twine.

The babe is more than swaddling bands;
Every farmer understands.
Every tear from every eye
Becomes a babe in eternity;

This is caught by females bright,
And return'd to its own delight.
The bleat, the bark, bellow, and roar,
Are waves that beat on heaven's shore.

The babe that weeps the rod beneath
Writes revenge in realms of death.
The beggar's rags, fluttering in air,
Does to rags the heavens tear.

The soldier, arm'd with sword and gun,
Palsied strikes the summer's sun.
The poor man's farthing is worth more
Than all the gold on Afric's shore.

One mite wrung from the lab'rer's hands
Shall buy and sell the miser's lands;

Or, if protected from on high,
Does that whole nation sell and buy.

He who mocks the infant's faith
Shall be mock'd in age and death.
He who shall teach the child to doubt
The rotting grave shall ne'er get out.

He who respects the infant's faith
Triumphs over hell and death.
The child's toys and the old man's reasons
Are the fruits of the two seasons.

The questioner, who sits so sly,
Shall never know how to reply.
He who replies to words of doubt
Doth put the light of knowledge out.

The strongest poison ever known
Came from Caesar's laurel crown.
Nought can deform the human race
Like to the armour's iron brace.

When gold and gems adorn the plow,
To peaceful arts shall envy bow.
A riddle, or the cricket's cry,
Is to doubt a fit reply.

The emmet's inch and eagle's mile
Make lame philosophy to smile.
He who doubts from what he sees
Will ne'er believe, do what you please.

If the sun and moon should doubt,
They'd immediately go out.

To be in a passion you good may do,
But no good if a passion is in you.

The whore and gambler, by the state
Licensed, build that nation's fate.
The harlot's cry from street to street
Shall weave old England's winding-sheet.

The winner's shout, the loser's curse,
Dance before dead England's hearse.

Every night and every morn
Some to misery are born,
Every morn and every night
Some are born to sweet delight.

Some are born to sweet delight,
Some are born to endless night.

We are led to believe a lie
When we see not thro' the eye,
Which was born in a night to perish in a night,
When the soul slept in beams of light.

God appears, and God is light,
To those poor souls who dwell in night;
But does a human form display
To those who dwell in realms of day.

This poem appeared in the Pickering Manuscript, a
notebook of William Blake's, and was thought to have been
written in 1803, although it was not published until 1863.

The Fifth of November
—Traditional

Remember, remember!
The fifth of November,
The Gunpowder treason and plot;
I know of no reason
Why the Gunpowder treason
Should ever be forgot!

Guy Fawkes and his companions
Did the scheme contrive,
To blow the King and Parliament
All up alive.

Threescore barrels, laid below,
To prove old England's overthrow.
But, by God's providence, him they catch,
With a dark lantern, lighting a match!

A stick and a stake
For King James's sake!
If you won't give me one,
I'll take two,
The better for me,
And the worse for you.

A rope, a rope, to hang the Pope,
A penn'orth of cheese to choke him,
A pint of beer to wash it down,
And a jolly good fire to burn him.

Holloa, boys! holloa, boys! make the bells ring!
Holloa, boys! holloa boys! God save the King!
Hip, hip, hooor-r-r-ray!

This version of the traditional English nursery rhyme is an amalgamation of several earlier nursery rhymes and is thought to date from 1870. It commemorates Guy Fawkes' failed attempt to blow up the House of Parliament on 5 November 1605, a day when the king, James VI of Scotland and I of England, was supposed to be present.

Leda and the Swan
—William Butler Yeats (1865-1939)

A sudden blow: the great wings beating still
Above the staggering girl, her thighs caressed
By the dark webs, her nape caught in his bill,
He holds her helpless breast upon his breast.

How can those terrified vague fingers push
The feathered glory from her loosening thighs?
And how can body, laid in that white rush,
But feel the strange heart beating where it lies?

A shudder in the loins engenders there
The broken wall, the burning roof and tower
And Agamemnon dead.

                          Being so caught up,
So mastered by the brute blood of the air,
Did she put on his knowledge with his power
Before the indifferent beak could let her drop?

Written in 1923, first published in *The Dial* magazine June
1924 and included in the collection *The Cat and the Moon
and Certain Poems,* 1924.

Ginevra
—Samuel Rogers (1763-1855)

If thou shouldst ever come by choice or chance
To Modena, where still religiously
Among her ancient trophies is preserved
Bologna's bucket (in its chain it hangs
Within that reverend tower, the Guirlandine)
Stop at a Palace near the Reggio-gate,
Dwelt in of old by one of the Orsini.
Its noble gardens, terrace above terrace,
And rich in fountains, statues, cypresses,
Will long detain thee; thro' their arched walks,
Dim at noon-day, discovering many a glimpse
Of knights and dames, such as in old romance,
And lovers, such as in heroic song,
Perhaps the two, for groves were their delight,
Who in the spring-time, as alone they sat,
Venturing together on a tale of love,
Read only part that day.—A summer-sun
Sets ere one half is seen; but ere thou go,
Enter the house—prythee, forget it not—
And look awhile upon a picture there.

'Tis of a Lady in her earliest youth,
The very last of that illustrious race,
Done by Zampieri—but by whom I care not.
He, who observes it—ere he passes on,
Gazes his fill, and comes and comes again,
That he may call it up, when far away.

She sits, inclining forward as to speak,
Her lips half-open, and her finger up,
As tho' she said 'Beware!' her vest of gold

Broidered with flowers, and clasped from head to
    foot,
An emerald-stone in every golden clasp;
And on her brow, fairer than alabaster,
A coronet of pearls.

But then her face,
So lovely, yet so arch, so full of mirth,
The overflowings of an innocent heart—
It haunts me still, tho' many a year has fled,
Like some wild melody!

Alone it hangs
Over a mouldering heir-loom, its companion,
An oaken-chest, half-eaten by the worm,
But richly carved by Antony of Trent
With scripture-stories from the Life of Christ;
A chest that came from Venice, and had held
The ducal robes of some old Ancestor.
That by the way—it may be true or false—
But don't forget the picture; and thou wilt not,
When thou hast heard the tale they told me there.

She was an only child; from infancy
The joy, the pride of an indulgent Sire.
Her Mother dying of the gift she gave,
That precious gift, what else remained to him?
The young Ginevra was his all in life,
Still as she grew, for ever in his sight;
And in her fifteenth year became a bride,
Marrying an only son, Francesco Doria,
Her playmate from her birth, and her first love.

Just as she looks there in her bridal dress,
She was all gentleness, all gaiety;

Her pranks the favourite theme of every tongue.
But now the day was come, the day, the hour:
Now, frowning, smiling, for the hundredth time,
The nurse, that ancient lady, preached decorum;
And, in the lustre of her youth, she gave
Her hand, with her heart in it, to Francesco.

Great was the joy; but at the Bridal feast,
When all sat down, the Bride was wanting there.
Nor was she to be found! Her Father cried,
' 'Tis but to make a trial of our love!'
And filled his glass to all; but his hand shook,
And soon from guest to guest the panic spread.
'Twas but that instant she had left Francesco,
Laughing and looking back and flying still,
Her ivory-tooth imprinted on his finger.
But now, alas, she was not to be found;
Nor from that hour could any thing be guessed,
But that she was not!

Weary of his life,
Francesco flew to Venice, and forthwith
Flung it away in battle with the Turk.
Orsini lived; and long might'st thou have seen
An old man wandering as in quest of something,
Something he could not find—he knew not what.
When he was gone, the house remained awhile
Silent and tenantless—then went to strangers.

Full fifty years were past, and all forgot,
When on an idle day, a day of search
'Mid the old lumber in the Gallery,
That mouldering chest was noticed; and 'twas said
By one as young, as thoughtless as Ginevra,
'Why not remove it from its lurking place?'

'Twas done as soon as said; but on the way
It burst, it fell; and lo, a skeleton,
With here and there a pearl, an emerald-stone,
A golden-clasp, clasping a shred of gold.
All else had perished—save a nuptial ring,
And a small seal, her mother's legacy,
Engraven with a name, the name of both,
'Ginevra.'

There then had she found a grave!
Within that chest had she concealed herself,
Fluttering with joy, the happiest of the happy;
When a spring-lock, that lay in ambush there,
Fastened her down for ever!

First published in 1823 in *Italy: A Poem, Volume 1*. This version is from the illustrated and revised edition published in 1830.

The Complaint of Chaucer to his Empty Purse
—Geoffrey Chaucer (?1340-1400)

To you, my purse, and to none other wight
Complain I, for ye be my lady dear!
I am so sorrow, now that ye be light;
For certes, but ye make me heavy cheer,
Me were as leif be laid upon my bier;
For which unto your mercy thus I cry:
Be heavy again, or elles might I die!

Now voucheth safe this day, or it be night,
That I of you the blissful sound may hear,
Or see your colour like the sun bright
That of yellowness had never a peer.
Ye be my life, ye be my hertes stere,
Queen of comfort an of good company:
Be heavy again, or elles might I die!

Now purse, that be to me my life's light,
And saviour, as down in this world here,
Out of this toune help me through your might,
Since that ye wole not be my treasurer;
For I am shaved as nigh as any frere.
But yet I pray unto your courtesy
Be heavy again, or elles might I die!

O Conqueror of Brute's Albion
Which that by line and free election
Be very king, this song to you I send;
And ye, that mighten all our harm amend,
Have mind upon my supplication!

Thought to have been the last poem Chaucer wrote and written by him to the king of the time (Henry IV) to remind him to pay his promised pension.

Home No More to Me
—Robert Louis Stevenson (1850-1894)

(To the tune of Wandering Willie)

Home no more home to me, whither must I
    wander?
Hunger my driver, I go where I must.
Cold blows the winter wind over hill and heather;
Thick drives the rain, and my roof is in the dust.
Loved of wise men was the shade of my roof-
    tree.
The true word of welcome was spoken in the
    door—
Dear days of old, with the faces in the firelight,
Kind folks of old, you come again no more.

Home was home then, my dear, full of kindly
    faces,
Home was home then, my dear, happy for the
    child.
Fire and the windows bright glittered on the
    moorland;
Song, tuneful song, built a palace in the wild.
Now, when day dawns on the brow of the
    moorland,
Lone stands the house, and the chimney-stone is
    cold.

Lone let is stand, now the friends are all
   departed,
The kind hearts, the true hearts, that loved the
   place of old.

Spring shall come, come again, calling up the
   moor-fowl,
Spring shall bring the sun and rain, bring the bees
   and flowers;
Red shall the heather bloom over hill and valley,
Soft flow the stream through the even-flowing
   hours;
Fair the day shine as it shone on my childhood—
Fair shine the day on the house with open door;
Birds come and cry there and twitter in the
   chimney—
But I go for ever and come again no more.

Published after the poet's death in *Songs of Travel and
Other Verses*, 1896.

Break of Day in the Trenches
—Isaac Rosenberg (1890-1918)

The darkness crumbles away
It is the same old druid Time as ever,
Only a live thing leaps my hand,
A queer sardonic rat,
As I pull the parapet's poppy
To stick behind my ear.
Droll rat, they would shoot you if they knew
Your cosmopolitan sympathies,
Now you have touched this English hand
You will do the same to a German
Soon, no doubt, if it be your pleasure
To cross the sleeping green between.
It seems you inwardly grin as you pass
Strong eyes, fine limbs, haughty athletes,
Less chanced than you for life,
Bonds to the whims of murder,
Sprawled in the bowels of the earth,
The torn fields of France.
What do you see in our eyes
At the shrieking iron and flame
Hurled through still heavens?
What quaver—what heart aghast?
Poppies whose roots are in men's veins
Drop, and are ever dropping;
But mine in my ear is safe—
Just a little white with the dust.

First published in *Poetry: A Magazine of Verse*, Volume IX, Number III, December 1916.

The Spider and the Fly
—Mary Howitt (1799-1888)

A new Version of an old Story.

'Will you walk into my parlour? said the Spider to the
    Fly,
'Tis the prettiest little parlour that ever you did spy;
The way into my parlour is up a winding stair,
And I've a many curious things to shew when you are
    there.'
'Oh no, no,' said the little Fly, 'to ask me is in vain,
For who goes up your winding stair can ne'er come
    down again.'

'I'm sure you must be weary, dear, with soaring up so
    high;
Will you rest upon my little bed?' said the Spider to
    the Fly.
'There are pretty curtains drawn around; the sheets
    are fine and thin,
And if you like to rest awhile, I'll snugly tuck you in!'
'Oh no, no,' said the little Fly, 'for I've often heard it
    said,
They never, never wake again, who sleep upon your
    bed!'

Said the cunning Spider to the Fly, 'Dear friend what
    can I do,
To prove the warm affection I've always felt for you?
I have within my pantry, good store of all that's nice;
I'm sure you're very welcome—will you please to take
    a slice?'

'Oh no, no,' said the little Fly, 'kind Sir, that cannot be,
I've heard what's in your pantry, and I do not wish to
    see!'

'Sweet creature!' said the Spider, 'you're witty and
    you're wise,
How handsome are your gauzy wings, how brilliant
    are your eyes!
I've a little looking-glass upon my parlour shelf,
If you'll step in one moment, dear, you shall behold
    yourself.'
'I thank you, gentle sir,' she said, 'for what you're
    pleased to say,
And bidding you good morning now, I'll call another
    day.'

The Spider turned him round about, and went into his
    den,
For well he knew the silly Fly would soon come back
    again:
So he wove a subtle web, in a little corner sly,
And set his table ready, to dine upon the Fly.
Then he came out to his door again, and merrily did
    sing,
'Come hither, hither, pretty Fly, with the pearl and
    silver wing;
Your robes are green and purple—there's a crest
    upon your head;
Your eyes are like the diamond bright, but mine are
    dull as lead!'

Alas, alas! how very soon this silly little Fly,
Hearing his wily, flattering words, came slowly flitting
    by;

With buzzing wings she hung aloft, then near and
    nearer drew,
Thinking only of her brilliant eyes, and green and
    purple hue—
Thinking only of her crested head—poor foolish thing!
    At last,
Up jumped the cunning Spider, and fiercely held her
    fast.
He dragged her up his winding stair, into his dismal
    den,
Within his little parlour—but she ne'er came out
    again!

And now dear little children, who may this story read,
To idle, silly flattering words, I pray you ne'er give
    heed:
Unto an evil counsellor, close heart and ear and eye,
And take a lesson from this tale, of the Spider and the
    Fly.

First published in *The New Year's Gift and Juvenile Souvenir*
for 1829.

Natural Comparisons with Perfect Love
—Edward Dyer (?1543-1607)

The lowest trees have tops, the ant her gall,
  The fly her spleen, the little sparks their heat;
The slender hairs cast shadows, though but small,
  And bees have stings, although they be not great;
Seas have their source, and so have shallow springs;
And love is love, in beggars as in kings.

Where rivers smoothest run, deep are the fords;
  The dial stirs, yet none perceives it move;
The firmest faith is in the fewest words;
  The turtles cannot sing, and yet they love:
True hearts have eyes and ears, no tongues to speak;
They hear and see, and sigh, and then they break.

First known appearance was in *Davison's Poetical Rhapsody*, first published in 1602, where it has the title used here. It is also known as 'A Modest Love'.

Ode On a Grecian Urn
—John Keats (1795-1821)

Thou still unravish'd bride of quietness,
   Thou foster-child of Silence and slow Time,
Sylvan historian, who canst thus express
   A flowery tale more sweetly than our rhyme:
What leaf-fringed legend haunts about thy shape
   Of deities or mortals, or of both,
In Tempe or the dales of Arcady?
   What men or gods are these? what maidens loth?
What mad pursuit? What struggle to escape?
   What pipes and timbrels? What wild ecstasy?

Heard melodies are sweet, but those unheard
   Are sweeter; therefore, ye soft pipes, play on;
Not to the sensual ear, but, more endear'd,
   Pipe to the spirit ditties of no tone:
Fair youth, beneath the trees, thou canst not leave
   Thy song, nor ever can those trees be bare;
Bold lover, never, never canst thou kiss,
   Though winning near the goal–yet, do not grieve;
She cannot fade, though thou hast not thy bliss,
   For ever wilt thou love, and she be fair!

Ah, happy, happy boughs! that cannot shed
   Your leaves, nor ever bid the Spring adieu;
And, happy melodist, unwearied,
   For ever piping songs for ever new;
More happy love! more happy, happy love!
   For ever warm and still to be enjoy'd,
For ever panting, and for ever young;
   All breathing human passion far above,

That leaves a heart high-sorrowful and cloy'd,
  A burning forehead, and a parching tongue.

Who are these coming to the sacrifice?
  To what green altar, O mysterious priest,
Lead'st thou that heifer lowing at the skies,
  And all her silken flanks with garlands drest?
What little town by river or sea shore,
  Or mountain-built with peaceful citadel,
Is emptied of this folk, this pious morn?
  And, little town, thy streets for evermore
Will silent be; and not a soul to tell
  Why thou art desolate, can e'er return.

O Attic shape! Fair attitude! with brede
  Of marble men and maidens overwrought,
With forest branches and the trodden weed;
  Thou, silent form, dost tease us out of thought
As doth eternity: Cold pastoral!
  When old age shall this generation waste,
Thou shalt remain, in midst of other woe
  Than ours, a friend to man, to whom thou say'st,
'Beauty is truth, truth beauty'—that is all
  Ye know on earth, and all ye need to know.

First published anonymously in *Annals of the Fine Arts for 1819,* Volume IV, Number 15, as 'On a Grecian Urn', and known to have been written in May 1819.

All That's Past
—Walter de la Mare (1873-1956)

Very old are the woods;
And the buds that break
Out of the brier's boughs,
When March winds wake,
So old with their beauty are—
Oh, no man knows
Through what wild centuries
Roves back the rose.

Very old are the brooks;
And the rills that rise
Where snow sleeps cold beneath
The azure skies
Sing such a history
Of come and gone,
Their every drop is as wise
As Solomon.

Very old are we men;
Our dreams are tales
Told in dim Eden
By Eve's nightingales;
We wake and whisper awhile,
But, the day gone by,
Silence and sleep like fields
Of amaranth lie.

Appeared in *The Listeners, and Other Poems*, first published
in 1912.

Westron Wind
—Anonymous

Westron wind, when will thou blow?
The small rain down can rain.
Christ, if my love were in my arms,
And I in my bed again.

First appeared in a songbook of 1530 but thought to be
much older.

On the Morning of Christ's Nativity
—John Milton (1608-1674)

I

This is the month, and this the happy morn
Wherein the Son of Heav'n's eternal King,
Of wedded Maid, and Virgin Mother born,
Our great redemption from above did bring;
For so the holy sages once did sing,
  That he our deadly forfeit should release,
And with his Father work us a perpetual peace.

II

That glorious Form, that Light unsufferable,
And that far-beaming blaze of Majesty,
Wherewith he wont at Heav'n's high council-table,
To sit the midst of Trinal Unity,
He laid aside, and here with us to be,
  Forsook the courts of everlasting day,
And chose with us a darksome house of mortal clay.

III

Say Heav'nly Muse, shall not thy sacred vein
Afford a present to the Infant God?
Hast thou no verse, no hymn, or solemn strain,
To welcome him to this his new abode,
Now while the heav'n, by the Sun's team untrod,
  Hath took no print of the approaching light,
And all the spangled host keep watch in squadrons
    bright?

IV

See how from far upon the eastern road
The star-led wizards haste with odours sweet:

O run, prevent them with thy humble ode,
And lay it lowly at his blessed feet;
Have thou the honour first thy Lord to greet,
  And join thy voice unto the angel quire,
From out his secret altar touched with hallowed fire.

The Hymn
I
It was the winter wild,
While the Heav'n-born child,
  All meanly wrapt in the rude manger lies;
Nature in awe to him
Had doffed her gaudy trim,
  With her great Master so to sympathize:
It was no season then for her
To wanton with the Sun, her lusty paramour.

II
Only with speeches fair
She woos the gentle air
  To hide her guilty front with innocent snow,
And on her naked shame,
Pollute with sinful blame,
  The saintly veil of maiden white to throw,
Confounded, that her Maker's eyes
Should look so near upon her foul deformities.

III
But he, her fears to cease,
Sent down the meek-eyed Peace:
  She, crowned with olive green, came softly sliding
Down through the turning sphere,
His ready harbinger,
  With turtle wing the amorous clouds dividing;

And waving wide her myrtle wand,
She strikes a universal peace through sea and land.

IV
No war or battle's sound
Was heard the world around;
  The idle spear and shield were high uphung;
The hooked chariot stood
Unstained with hostile blood;
  The trumpet spake not to the armed throng;
And kings sate still with awful eye,
  As if they surely knew their sovran Lord was by.

V
But peaceful was the night
Wherein the Prince of Light
  His reign of peace upon the earth began:
The winds with wonder whist,
Smoothly the waters kist,
  Whispering new joys to the mild Ocean,
Who now hath quite forgot to rave,
While birds of calm sit brooding on the charmed
        wave.

VI
The Stars with deep amaze
Stand fixed in steadfast gaze,
  Bending one way their precious influence;
And will not take their flight,
For all the morning light,
  Or Lucifer that often warned them thence,
But in their glimmering orbs did glow,
Until their Lord himself bespake, and bid them go.

VI
And though the shady gloom
Had given day her room,
  The Sun himself withheld his wonted speed,
And hid his head for shame,
As his inferior flame
  The new-enlightened world no more should need:
He saw a greater Sun appear
Than his bright throne or burning axle-tree could
    bear.

VIII
The shepherds on the lawn,
Or ere the point of dawn,
  Sate simply chatting in a rustic row;
Full little thought they than
That the mighty Pan
  Was kindly come to live with them below:
Perhaps their loves, or else their sheep,
Was all that did their silly thoughts so busy keep;

IX
When such music sweet
Their hearts and ears did greet,
  As never was by mortal finger strook,
Divinely warbled voice
Answering the stringed noise,
  As all their souls in blissful rapture took:
The air such pleasure loth to lose,
With thousand echoes still prolongs each heav'nly
    close.

X
Nature, that heard such sound
Beneath the hollow round

Of Cynthia's seat, the Airy region thrilling,
Now was almost won
To think her part was done,
  And that her reign had here its last fulfilling:
She knew such harmony alone
Could hold all heav'n and earth in happier union.

XI
At last surrounds their sight
A globe of circular light,
  That with long beams the shame-faced Night
    arrayed;
The helmed Cherubim
And sworded Seraphim
  Are seen in glittering ranks with wings displayed,
Harping in loud and solemn quire,
With unexpressive notes to Heav'n's new-born Heir.

XII
Such music (as 'tis said)
Before was never made,
  But when of old the sons of morning sung,
While the Creator great
His constellations set,
  And the well-balanced world on hinges hung,
And cast the dark foundations deep,
And bid the welt'ring waves their oozy channel keep.

XIII
Ring out ye crystal spheres!
Once bless our human ears
  (If ye have power to touch our senses so)
And let your silver chime
Move in melodious time,
  And let the bass of Heav'n's deep organ blow;

And with your ninefold harmony
Make up full consort to th'angelic symphony.

XIV
For if such holy song
Enwrap our fancy long,
  Time will run back and fetch the age of gold,
And speckled Vanity
Will sicken soon and die,
  And leprous Sin will melt from earthly mould;
And Hell itself will pass away,
And leave her dolorous mansions to the peering Day.

XV
Yea, Truth and Justice then
Will down return to men,
  Orbed in a rainbow; and, like glories wearing,
Mercy will sit between,
Throned in celestial sheen,
  With radiant feet the tissued clouds down steering;
And Heav'n, as at some festival,
Will open wide the gates of her high palace hall.

XVI
But wisest Fate says no:
This must not yet be so;
  The Babe lies yet in smiling infancy,
That on the bitter cross
Must redeem our loss,
  So both himself and us to glorify:
Yet first to those ychained in sleep,
The wakeful trump of doom must thundcr through
    the deep,

XVII

With such a horrid clang
As on Mount Sinai rang
  While the red fire and smould'ring clouds outbrake:
The aged Earth, aghast
With terror of that blast,
  Shall from the surface to the centre shake,
When at the world's last session,
The dreadful Judge in middle air shall spread his
    throne.

XVIII

And then at last our bliss
Full and perfect is,
  But now begins; for from this happy day
Th'old Dragon under ground,
In straiter limits bound,
  Not half so far casts his usurped sway,
And, wrath to see his kingdom fall,
Swinges the scaly horror of his folded tail.

XIX

The Oracles are dumb;
No voice or hideous hum
  Runs through the arched roof in words deceiving.
Apollo from his shrine
Can no more divine,
  With hollow shriek the steep of Delphos leaving.
No nightly trance or breathed spell
Inspires the pale-eyed priest from the prophetic cell.

XX

The lonely mountains o'er,
And the resounding shore,
  A voice of weeping heard and loud lament;

From haunted spring, and dale
Edged with poplar pale,
    The parting Genius is with sighing sent;
With flow'r-inwoven tresses torn
The Nymphs in twilight shade of tangled thickets
    mourn.

XXI
In consecrated earth,
And on the holy hearth,
    The Lars and Lemures moan with midnight plaint;
In urns and altars round,
A drear and dying sound
    Affrights the flamens at their service quaint;
And the chill marble seems to sweat,
While each peculiar power forgoes his wonted seat.

XXII
Peor and Baalim
Forsake their temples dim,
    With that twice-battered god of Palestine;
And mooned Ashtaroth,
Heav'n's queen and mother both,
    Now sits not girt with tapers' holy shine;
The Libyc Hammon shrinks his horn;
In vain the Tyrian maids their wounded Thammuz
    mourn.

XXIII
And sullen Moloch, fled,
Hath left in shadows dread
    His burning idol all of blackest hue:
In vain with cymbals' ring
They call the grisly king,
    In dismal dance about the furnace blue.

The brutish gods of Nile as fast,
Isis and Orus, and the dog Anubis, haste.

XXIV
Nor is Osiris seen
In Memphian grove or green,
  Trampling the unshower'd grass with lowings loud;
Nor can he be at rest
Within his sacred chest,
  Naught but profoundest Hell can be his shroud:
In vain with timbreled anthems dark
The sable-stoled sorcerers bear his worshipped ark.

XXV
He feels from Juda's land
The dreaded Infant's hand,
  The rays of Bethlehem blind his dusky eyn;
Nor all the gods beside
Longer dare abide,
  Not Typhon huge ending in snaky twine:
Our Babe, to show his Godhead true,
Can in his swaddling bands control the damned crew.

XXVI
So when the Sun in bed,
Curtained with cloudy red,
  Pillows his chin upon an orient wave,
The flocking shadows pale
Troop to th'infernal jail,
  Each fettered ghost slips to his several grave,
And the yellow-skirted fays
Fly after the night-steeds, leaving their moon-loved
    maze.

XXVII
But see, the Virgin blest
Hath laid her Babe to rest:
  Time is our tedious song should here have ending.
Heav'n's youngest-teemed star,
Hath fixed her polished car,
  Her sleeping Lord with handmaid lamp attending;
And all about the courtly stable,
Bright-harnessed Angels sit in order serviceable.

Written in 1629 but not published until 1645 in *Poems of Mr. John Milton, Both English and Latin, Compos'd at several times.*

Fire and Ice
—Robert Frost (1874-1963)

Some say the world will end in fire,
Some say in ice.
From what I've tasted of desire
I hold with those who favour fire.
But if it had to perish twice,
I think I know enough of hate
To say that for destruction ice
Is also great
And would suffice.

First appeared in *Harper's Magazine*, December 1920.

My True Love Hath My Heart
—Philip Sidney (1554-1586)

My true love hath my heart and I have his,
By just exchange one for the other given:
I hold his dear, and mine he cannot miss;
There never was a bargain better driven.
His heart in me keeps me and him in one;
My heart in him his thoughts and senses guides:
He loves my heart, for once it was his own;
I cherish his because in me it bides.
His heart his wound received from my sight;
My heart was wounded with his wounded heart;
For as from me on him his hurt did light,
So still, methought, in me his hurt did smart:
Both equal hurt, in this change sought our bliss,
My true love hath my heart and I have his.

This sonnet appeared in *The Countess of Pembroke's Arcadia* which was unfinished at the poet's death. It was first published in 1590.

The Raven
—Edgar Allan Poe (1809-1849)

Once upon a midnight dreary, while I pondered, weak
    and weary,
Over many a quaint and curious volume of forgotten
    lore,
While I nodded, nearly napping, suddenly there came
    a tapping,
As of someone gently rapping, rapping at my chamber
    door.
' 'Tis some visitor,' I muttered, 'tapping at my
    chamber door;
Only this, and nothing more.'

Ah, distinctly I remember, it was in the bleak
    December,
And each separate dying ember wrought its ghost
    upon the floor.
Eagerly I wished the morrow; vainly I had sought to
    borrow
From my books surcease of sorrow, sorrow for the
    lost Lenore,
For the rare and radiant maiden whom the angels
    name Lenore,
Nameless here forevermore.

And the silken sad uncertain rustling of each purple
    curtain
Thrilled me—filled me with fantastic terrors never felt
    before;
So that now, to still the beating of my heart, I stood
    repeating,

' 'Tis some visitor entreating entrance at my chamber
    door,
Some late visitor entreating entrance at my chamber
    door.
This it is, and nothing more.'

Presently my soul grew stronger; hesitating then no
    longer,
'Sir,' said I, 'or madam, truly your forgiveness I
    implore;
But the fact is, I was napping, and so gently you came
    rapping,
And so faintly you came tapping, tapping at my
    chamber door,
That I scarce was sure I heard you.' Here I opened
    wide the door;—
Darkness there, and nothing more.

Deep into the darkness peering, long I stood there,
    wondering, fearing
Doubting, dreaming dreams no mortals ever dared to
    dream before;
But the silence was unbroken, and the stillness gave
    no token,
And the only word there spoken was the whispered
    word,
Lenore?, This I whispered, and an echo murmured
    back the word,
'Lenore!' Merely this, and nothing more.

Back into the chamber turning, all my soul within me
    burning,
Soon again I heard a tapping, something louder than
    before,

'Surely,' said I, 'surely, that is something at my
   window lattice.
Let me see, then, what thereat is, and this mystery
   explore.
Let my heart be still a moment, and this mystery
   explore.
' 'Tis the wind, and nothing more.'

Open here I flung the shutter, when, with many a flirt
   and flutter,
In there stepped a stately raven, of the saintly days of
   yore.
Not the least obeisance made he; not a minute
   stopped or stayed he;
But with mien of lord or lady, perched above my
   chamber door.
Perched upon a bust of Pallas, just above my chamber
   door,
Perched, and sat, and nothing more.

Then this ebony bird beguiling my sad fancy into
   smiling,
By the grave and stern decorum of the countenance it
   wore,
'Though thy crest be shorn and shaven thou,' I said,
   'art sure no craven,
Ghastly, grim, and ancient raven, wandering from the
   nightly shore.
Tell me what the lordly name is on the Night's
   Plutonian shore.'
Quoth the raven, 'Nevermore.'

Much I marvelled this ungainly fowl to hear discourse
    so plainly,
Though its answer little meaning, little relevancy
    bore;
For we cannot help agreeing that no living human
    being
Ever yet was blessed with seeing bird above his
    chamber door,
Bird or beast upon the sculptured bust above his
    chamber door,
With such name as 'Nevermore.'

But the raven, sitting lonely on that placid bust, spoke
    only
That one word, as if his soul in that one word he did
    outpour.
Nothing further then he uttered; not a feather then
    he fluttered;
Till I scarcely more than muttered, 'Other friends have
    flown before;
On the morrow he will leave me, as my hopes have
    flown before.'
Then the bird said, 'Nevermore.'

Startled at the stillness broken by reply so aptly
    spoken,
'Doubtless,' said I, 'what it utters is its only stock and
    store,
Caught from some unhappy master, whom unmerciful
    disaster
Followed fast and followed faster, till his songs one
    burden bore,—
Till the dirges of his hope that melancholy burden
    bore
Of 'Never—nevermore.'

But the raven still beguiling all my sad soul into
    smiling,
Straight I wheeled a cushioned seat in front of bird,
    and bust and door;
Then, upon the velvet sinking, I betook myself to
    linking
Fancy unto fancy, thinking what this ominous bird of
    yore —
What this grim, ungainly, ghastly, gaunt and ominous
    bird of yore
Meant in croaking 'Nevermore.'

Thus I sat engaged in guessing, but no syllable
    expressing
To the fowl, whose fiery eyes now burned into my
    bosom's core;
This and more I sat divining, with my head at ease
    reclining
On the cushion's velvet lining that the lamplight
    gloated o'er,
But whose velvet violet lining with the lamplight
    gloating o'er
She shall press, ah, nevermore!

Then, methought, the air grew denser, perfumed
    from an unseen censer
Swung by seraphim whose footfalls tinkled on the
    tufted floor.
'Wretch,' I cried, 'thy God hath lent thee — by these
    angels he hath
Sent thee respite—respite and nepenthe from thy
    memories of Lenore!

Quaff, O quaff this kind nepenthe, and forget this lost
   Lenore!'
Quoth the raven, 'Nevermore!'

'Prophet!' said I, 'thing of evil!–prophet still, if bird or
   devil!
Whether tempter sent, or whether tempest tossed
   thee here ashore,
Desolate, yet all undaunted, on this desert land
   enchanted–
On this home by horror haunted–tell me truly, I
   implore:
Is there–is there balm in Gilead?–tell me–tell me I
   implore!'
Quoth the raven, 'Nevermore.'

'Prophet!' said I, 'thing of evil–prophet still, if bird or
   devil!
By that heaven that bends above us–by that God we
   both adore–
Tell this soul with sorrow laden, if, within the distant
   Aidenn,
It shall clasp a sainted maiden, whom the angels
   name Lenore—
Clasp a rare and radiant maiden, whom the angels
   name Lenore?
Quoth the raven, 'Nevermore.'

'Be that word our sign of parting, bird or fiend!' I
   shrieked, upstarting–
'Get thee back into the tempest and the Night's
   Plutonian shore!
Leave no black plume as a token of that lie thy soul
   hath spoken!

Leave my loneliness unbroken! — quit the bust above
    my door!
Take thy beak from out my heart, and take thy form
    from off my door!'
Quoth the raven, 'Nevermore.'

And the raven, never flitting, still is sitting, still is
    sitting
On the pallid bust of Pallas just above my chamber
    door;
And his eyes have all the seeming of a demon's that is
    dreaming.
And the lamplight o'er him streaming throws his
    shadow on the floor;
And my soul from out that shadow that lies floating
    on the floor
Shall be lifted—nevermore!

First published in January 1845.

Said Hanrahan
—John O'Brien (Patrick Joseph Hartigan) (1878-1952)

'We'll all be rooned,' said Hanrahan,
    In accents most forlorn,
Outside the church, ere Mass began,
    One frosty Sunday morn.

The congregation stood about,
    Coat-collars to the ears,
And talked of stock, and crops, and drought,
    As it had done for years.

'It's looking crook,' said Daniel Croke;
    'Bedad, it's cruke, me lad,
For never since the banks went broke
    Has seasons been so bad.'

'It's dry, all right,' said young O'Neil,
    With which astute remark
He squatted down upon his heel
    And chewed a piece of bark.

And so around the chorus ran
    'It's keepin' dry, no doubt.'
'We'll all be rooned,' said Hanrahan,
    'Before the year is out.'

'The crops are done; ye'll have your work
    To save one bag of grain;

From here way out to Back-o'-Bourke
    They're singin' out for rain.

'They're singin' out for rain,' he said,
    'And all the tanks are dry.'
The congregation scratched its head,
    And gazed around the sky.

'There won't be grass, in any case,
    Enough to feed an ass;
There's not a blade on Casey's place
    As I came down to Mass.'

'If rain don't come this month,' said Dan,
    And cleared his throat to speak —
'We'll all be rooned,' said Hanrahan,
    'If rain don't come this week.'

A heavy silence seemed to steal
    On all at this remark;
And each man squatted on his heel,
    And chewed a piece of bark.

'We want an inch of rain, we do,'
    O'Neil observed at last;
But Croke 'maintained' we wanted two
    To put the danger past.

'If we don't get three inches, man,
    Or four to break this drought,
We'll all be rooned,' said Hanrahan,
    'Before the year is out.'

In God's good time down came the rain;
    And all the afternoon
On iron roof and window-pane
    It drummed a homely tune.

And through the night it pattered still,
    And lightsome, gladsome elves
On dripping spout and window-sill
    Kept talking to themselves.

It pelted, pelted all day long,
    A-singing at its work,
Till every heart took up the song
    Way out to Back-o'-Bourke.

And every creek a banker ran,
    And dams filled overtop;
'We'll all be rooned,' said Hanrahan,
    'If this rain doesn't stop.'

And stop it did, in God's good time;
    And spring came in to fold
A mantle o'er the hills sublime
    Of green and pink and gold.

And days went by on dancing feet,
    With harvest-hopes immense,
And laughing eyes beheld the wheat
    Nid-nodding o'er the fence.

And, oh, the smiles on every face,
    As happy lad and lass
Through grass knee-deep on Casey's place
    Went riding down to Mass.

While round the church in clothes genteel
    Discoursed the men of mark,
And each man squatted on his heel,
    And chewed his piece of bark.

'There'll be bush-fires for sure, me man,
    There will, without a doubt;
We'll all be rooned,' said Hanrahan,
    'Before the year is out.'

First known publication in *The Catholic Press* in July 1919
and then appeared in the anthology *Around the Boree Log
and Other Verses*, 1921.

Ask Me No More
—Thomas Carew (1595–?1645)

Ask me no more where Jove bestows,
When June is past, the fading rose;
For in your beauty's orient deep
These flowers, as in their causes, sleep.

Ask me no more whither do stray
The golden atoms of the day;
For in pure love heaven did prepare
Those powders to enrich your hair.

Ask me no more whither doth haste
The nightingale when May is past;
For in your sweet dividing throat
She winters and keeps warm her note.

Ask me no more where those stars 'light
That downwards fall in dead of night;
For in your eyes they sit, and there
Fixed become as in their sphere.

Ask me no more if east or west
The Phoenix builds her spicy nest;
For unto you at last she flies,
And in your fragrant bosom dies.

First published in 1640 and edited in 1642.

Ye Wearie Wayfarer: Fytte VIII—Finis Exoptatus
—Adam Lindsay Gordon (1833-1870)

[A Metaphysical Song]

"There's something in this world amiss
Shall be unriddled by-and-bye."—Tennyson

Boot and saddle, see the slanting
  Rays begin to fall,
Flinging lights and colours flaunting
  Through the shadows tall,
Onward! onward! must we travel?
  When will come the goal?
Riddle I may not unravel,
  Cease to vex my soul.

Harshly break those peals of laughter
  From the jays aloft,
Can we guess what they cry after,
  We have heard them oft;
Perhaps some strain of rude thanksgiving
  Mingles in their song,
Are they glad that they are living?
  Are they right or wrong?
Right, 'tis joy that makes them call so,
  Why should they be sad?
Certes! we are living also,
  Shall not we be glad?
Onward! onward! must we travel?
  Is the goal more near?
Riddle we may not unravel,
  Why so dark and drear?

Yon small bird his hymn outpouring
  On the branch close by
Recks not for the kestrel soaring
  In the nether sky,
Though the hawk with wings extended
  Poises overhead,
Motionless as though suspended
  By a viewless thread.
See, he stoops, nay, shooting forward
  With the arrow's flight,
Swift and straight away to nor'ward
  Sails he out of sight.
Onward! onward! thus we travel,
  Comes the goal more nigh?
Riddle we may not unravel,
  Who shall make reply?

Ha! Friend Ephraim, saint or sinner,
  Tell me if you can—
Tho' we may not judge the inner
  By the outer man,
Yet by girth of broadcloth ample,
  And by cheeks that shine,
Surely you set no example
  In the fasting line—

Could you, like yon bird, discov'ring
  Fate, as close at hand
As the kestrel o'er him hov'ring,
  Still, as he did, stand?
Trusting grandly, singing gaily,
  Confident and calm,
Not one false note in your daily<
  Hymn or weekly psalm?

Oft your oily tones are heard in
  Chapel, where you preach,
This the everlasting burden
  Of the tale you teach:
"We are d—d, our sins are deadly,
  You alone are heal'd"—
'Twas not thus their gospel redly
  Saints and martyrs seal'd—
You had seem'd more like a martyr
  Than you seem to us,
To the beasts that caught a Tartar
  Once at Ephesus;
Rather than the stout apostle
  Of the Gentiles, who,
Pagan-like, could cuff and wrestle,
  They'd have chosen you.

Yet I ween on such occasion
  Your dissenting voice
Would have been, in mild persuasion,
  Raised against their choice;
Man of peace, and man of merit,
  Pompous, wise, and grave,
Ephraim! Is it flesh or spirit
  You strive most to save?
Vain is half this care and caution<
  O'er the earthly shell,
We can neither baffle nor shun
  Dark-plumed Azrael.
Onward! onward! still we wonder,
  Nearer draws the goal;
Half the riddle's read, we ponder
  Vainly on the whole.

Eastward! in the pink horizon,
  Fleecy hillocks shame
This dim range dull earth that lies on
  Tinged with rosy flame.
Westward! as a stricken giant
  Stoops his bloody crest,
And, tho' vanquished, frowns defiant,
  Sinks the sun to rest.
Distant yet, approaching quickly,
  From the shades that lurk,
Like a black pall gathers thickly
  Night, when none may work,
Soon our restless occupation
  Shall have ceased to be;
Units! in God's vast creation,
  Ciphers! what are we?
Onward! onward! oh! faint-hearted;
  Nearer and more near
Has the goal drawn since we started,
  Be of better cheer.

Preacher! all forbearance ask, for
  All are worthless found,
Man must aye take man to task for
  Faults while earth goes round.
On this dank soil thistles muster,
  Thorns are broadcast sown,
Seek not figs where thistles cluster,
  Grapes where thorns have grown.

Sun and rain and dew from heaven,
  Light and shade and air,
Heat and moisture freely given,
  Thorns and thistles share.

Vegetation rank and rotten
  Feels the cheering ray;
Not uncared for, unforgotten,
  We too have our day.

Unforgotten! though we cumber
  Earth, we work His will.
Shall we sleep through night's long slumber
  Unforgotten still?
Onward! onward! toiling ever,
  Weary steps and slow,
Doubting oft, despairing never,
  To the goal we go!

Hark! the bells on distant cattle
  Waft across the range,
Through the golden-tufted wattle,
  Music low and strange;
Like the marriage peal of fairies
  Comes the tinkling sound,
Or like chimes of sweet St. Mary's
  On far English ground.
How my courser champs the snaffle,
  And with nostril spread,
Snorts and scarcely seems to ruffle
  Fern leaves with his tread;
Cool and pleasant on his haunches
  Blows the evening breeze,
Through the overhanging branches
  Of the wattle trees:
Onward! to the Southern Ocean,
  Glides the breath of Spring.

Onward, with a dreamy motion,
  I, too, glide and sing—

Forward! forward! still we wander—
  Tinted hills that lie
In the red horizon yonder—
  Is the goal so nigh?

Whisper, spring-wind, softly singing,
  Whisper in my ear;
Respite and nepenthe bringing,
  Can the goal be near?
Laden with the dew of vespers,
  From the fragrant sky,
In my ear the wind that whispers
  Seems to make reply—

"Question not, but live and labour
  Till yon goal be won,
Helping every feeble neighbour,
  Seeking help from none;
Life is mostly froth and bubble,
  Two things stand like stone,
KINDNESS in another's trouble,
  COURAGE in your own."

Courage, comrades, this is certain,
  All is for the best—
There are lights behind the curtain—
  Gentles, let us rest,
As the smoke-rack veers to seaward,
  From 'the ancient clay',
With its moral drifting leeward,
  Ends the wanderer's lay.

Published in *Sea Spray and Smoke Drift*, 1867, as the eighth
and final 'fytte' of 'Ye Wearie Wayfarer. Hys Ballad'.

She Walks in Beauty
—George Gordon Byron (1788-1824)

She walks in beauty, like the night
  Of cloudless climes and starry skies;
And all that 's best of dark and bright
  Meet in her aspect and her eyes:
Thus mellow'd to that tender light
  Which heaven to gaudy day denies.

One shade the more, one ray the less,
  Had half impair'd the nameless grace
Which waves in every raven tress,
  Or softly lightens o'er her face;
Where thoughts serenely sweet express
  How pure, how dear their dwelling-place.

And on that cheek, and o'er that brow,
  So soft, so calm, yet eloquent,
The smiles that win, the tints that glow,
  But tell of days in goodness spent,
A mind at peace with all below,
  A heart whose love is innocent!

Written in 1814.

My Country
—Dorothea Mackellar (1885-1968)

The love of field and coppice,
Of green and shaded lanes.
Of ordered woods and gardens
Is running in your veins,
Strong love of grey-blue distance
Brown streams and soft dim skies
I know but cannot share it,
My love is otherwise.

I love a sunburnt country,
A land of sweeping plains,
Of ragged mountain ranges,
Of droughts and flooding rains.
I love her far horizons,
I love her jewel-sea,
Her beauty and her terror—
The wide brown land for me!

A stark white ring-barked forest
All tragic to the moon,
The sapphire-misted mountains,
The hot gold hush of noon.
Green tangle of the brushes,
Where lithe lianas coil,
And orchids deck the tree-tops
And ferns the warm dark soil.

Core of my heart, my country!
Her pitiless blue sky,
When sick at heart, around us,
We see the cattle die—

But then the grey clouds gather,
And we can bless again
The drumming of an army,
The steady, soaking rain.

Core of my heart, my country!
Land of the Rainbow Gold,
For flood and fire and famine,
She pays us back threefold—
Over the thirsty paddocks,
Watch, after many days,
The filmy veil of greenness
That thickens as we gaze.

An opal-hearted country,
A wilful, lavish land—
All you who have not loved her,
You will not understand—
Though earth holds many splendours,
Wherever I may die,
I know to what brown country
My homing thoughts will fly.

Written in 1904.

The World
—Henry Vaughan (1621-1695)

I saw Eternity the other night
Like a great Ring of pure and endless light
     All calm as it was bright;
And round beneath it, Time, in hours, days, years,
     Driven by the spheres,
Like a vast shadow moved, in which the world
     And all her train were hurled.
The doting Lover in his quaintest strain
     Did there complain;
Near him, his lute, his fancy, and his flights,
     Wit's sour delights;
With gloves and knots, the silly snares of pleasure;
     Yet his dear treasure
All scattered lay, while he his eyes did pour
     Upon a flower.

The darksome Statesman hung with weights and woe,
Like a thick midnight fog, moved there so slow
     He did nor stay nor go;
Condemning thoughts, like sad eclipses, scowl
     Upon his soul,
And clouds of crying witnesses without
     Pursued him with one shout.
Yet digged the mole, and, lest his ways be found,
     Worked under ground,
Where he did clutch his prey; but One did see
     That policy.
Churches and altars fed him, perjuries
     Were gnats and flies;
It rained about him blood and tears, but he
     Drank them as free.

The fearful Miser on a heap of rust
Sat pining all his life there, did scarce trust
   His own hands with the dust;
Yet would not place one piece above, but lives
   In fear of thieves.
Thousands there were as frantic as himself,
   And hugged each one his pelf.
The downright Epicure placed heaven in sense
   And scorned pretence;
While others, slipped into a wide excess,
   Said little less;
The weaker sort, slight, trivial wares enslave,
   Who think them brave;
And poor despisèd Truth sat counting by
   Their victory.

Yet some, who all this while did weep and sing,
And sing and weep, soared up into the Ring;
   But most would use no wing.
'Oh, fools,' said I, 'thus to prefer dark night
   Before true light,
To live in grots and caves, and hate the day
   Because it shows the way,
The way which from this dead and dark abode
   Leaps up to God,
A way where you might tread the sun, and be
   More bright than he.'
But as I did their madness so discuss,
   One whispered thus,
'This Ring the Bridegroom did for none provide
   But for his Bride.'

John Cap. 2. ver. 16, 17.
All that is in the world, the lust of the flesh, the lust of
the eyes, and the pride of life, is not of the Father,
but is of the world.
And the world passeth away, and the lusts thereof;
but he that doeth the will of God abideth for ever.

First published in *Silex Scintillans, or, Sacred Poems and Private Ejaculations*, 1650.

My Last Duchess
—Robert Browning (1812-1889)

Ferrara

That's my last Duchess painted on the wall,
Looking as if she were alive. I call
That piece a wonder, now: Frà Pandolf's hands
Worked busily a day, and there she stands.
Will't please you sit and look at her? I said
'Frà Pandolf' by design, for never read
Strangers like you that pictured countenance,
The depth and passion of its earnest glance,
But to myself they turned (since none puts by
The curtain I have drawn for you, but I)
And seemed as they would ask me, if they durst,
How such a glance came there; so, not the first
Are you to turn and ask thus. Sir, 'twas not
Her husband's presence only, called that spot
Of joy into the Duchess' cheek: perhaps
Frà Pandolf chanced to say "Her mantle laps
Over my Lady's wrist too much," or "Paint
Must never hope to reproduce the faint
Half-flush that dies along her throat": such stuff
Was courtesy, she thought, and cause enough
For calling up that spot of joy. She had
A heart—how shall I say?—too soon made glad,
Too easily impressed; she liked whate'er
She looked on, and her looks went everywhere.
Sir, 'twas all one! My favour at her breast,
The dropping of the daylight in the West,
The bough of cherries some officious fool
Broke in the orchard for her, the white mule
She rode with round the terrace—all and each

Would draw from her alike the approving speech,
Or blush, at least. She thanked men,—good! but
    thanked
Somehow—I know not how—as if she ranked
My gift of a nine-hundred-years-old name
With anybody's gift. Who'd stoop to blame
This sort of trifling? Even had you skill
In speech—(which I have not)—to make your will
Quite clear to such an one, and say, "Just this
Or that in you disgusts me; here you miss,
Or there exceed the mark"—and if she let
Herself be lessoned so, nor plainly set
Her wits to yours, forsooth, and made excuse,
—E'en then would be some stooping, and I choose
Never to stoop. Oh sir, she smiled, no doubt,
Whene'er I passed her; but who passed without
Much the same smile? This grew; I gave commands;
Then all smiles stopped together. There she stands
As if alive. Will't please you rise? We'll meet
The company below, then. I repeat,
The Count your master's known munificence
Is ample warrant that no just pretence
Of mine for dowry will be disallowed;
Though his fair daughter's self, as I avowed
At starting, is my object. Nay, we'll go
Together down, sir. Notice Neptune, though,
Taming a sea-horse, thought a rarity,
Which Claus of Innsbruck cast in bronze for me!

First published in *Dramatic Lyrics*, 1842, where it was
entitled 'Italy'.

Hope
—Emily Brontë (1818-1848)

Hope was but a timid friend;
She sat without the grated den,
Watching how my fate would tend,
Even as selfish-hearted men.

She was cruel in her fear;
Through the bars one dreary day,
I looked out to see her there,
And she turned her face away!

Like a false guard, false watch keeping,
Still, in strife, she whispered peace;
She would sing while I was weeping;
If I listened, she would cease.

False she was, and unrelenting;
When my last joys strewed the ground,
Even Sorrow saw, repenting,
Those sad relics scattered round;

Hope, whose whisper would have given
Balm to all my frenzied pain,
Stretched her wings, and soared to heaven,
Went, and ne'er returned again!

First published in *Poems by Currer, Ellis and Acton Bell* in 1846.

To Mistress Margaret Hussey
—John Skelton (?1460-1529)

Merry Margaret,
As midsummer flower,
Gentle as falcon
Or hawk of the tower;

With solace and gladness,
Much mirth and no madness,
All good and no badness,
So joyously,
So maidenly,
So womanly
Her demeaning
In every thing,
Far, far passing
That I can indite
Or suffice to write
Of Merry Margaret,
As midsummer flower,
Gentle as falcon
Or hawk of the tower;

As patient and as still
And as full of good will
As fair Isaphill,
Coriander,
Sweet pomander,
Good Cassander;
Steadfast of thought,
Well made, well wrought;
Far may be sought
Ere that ye can find

So courteous, so kind
As Merry Margaret,
This midsummer flower,
Gentle as falcon
Or hawk of the tower.

Published in 1523 in *The Garland of Laurel*.

Sea-Fever
—John Masefield (1878-1967)

I must down to the seas again, to the lonely sea and
the sky,
And all I ask is a tall ship and a star to steer her by,
And the wheel's kick and the wind's song and the
white sail's shaking,
And a grey mist on the sea's face, and a grey dawn
breaking.

I must down to the seas again, for the call of the
running tide
Is a wild call and a clear call that may not be denied;
And all I ask is a windy day with the white clouds
flying,
And the flung spray and the blown spume, and the
sea-gulls crying.

I must down to the seas again, to the vagrant gypsy
life,
To the gull's way and the whale's way where the
wind's like a whetted knife;
And all I ask is a merry yarn from a laughing fellow-
rover
And quiet sleep and a sweet dream when the long
trick's over.

First published in *Salt-Water Ballads*, 1902.

Idea LXI
—Michael Drayton (1563-1631)

Since there's no help, come let us kiss and part.
Nay, I have done, you get no more of me;
And I am glad, yea glad with all my heart,
That thus so cleanly I myself can free.
Shake hands for ever, cancel all our vows,
And when we meet at any time again,
Be it not seen in either of our brows
That we one jot of former love retain.
Now at the last gasp of Love's latest breath,
When, his pulse failing, Passion speechless lies;
When Faith is kneeling by his bed of death,
And Innocence is closing up his eyes—
Now, if thou wouldst, when all have given him over,
From death to life thou might'st him yet recover!

Published in 1619 in *Idea*.

Prologue. By A Gentleman of Leicester
—Henry Carter (?-1806)

*On opening the Theatre, at Sydney, Botany Bay, to be
spoken by the celebrated Mr Barrington*

From distant climes o'er wide-spread seas we come,
Though not with much eclat or beat of drum,
True patriots all; for be it understood,
We left our country for our country's good;
No private views disgrac'd our generous zeal,
What urg'd our travels was our country's weal;
And none will doubt but that our emigration
Has prov'd most useful to the British nation.

But, you inquire, what could our breasts inflame
With this new passion for theatric fame?
What, in the practice of our former days,
Could shape our talents to exhibit plays?
Your patience, sirs, some observations made,
You'll grant us equal to the scenic trade.

He, who to midnight ladders is no stranger,
You'll own will make an admirable Ranger.
To seek Macheath, we have not far to roam;
And sure in Filch I shall be quite at home.
Unrival'd there, none will dispute my claim
To high pre-eminence and exalted fame.

As oft on Gadshill we have ta'en our stand,
When 'twas so dark you could not see your hand,
Some true-bred Falstaff we may hope to start
Who, when well bolster'd, well will play his part.
The scene to vary, we shall try in time

To treat you with a little pantomime.
Here light and easy Columbines are found,
And well tried harlequins with us abound;
From durance vile our precious selves to keep,
We often had recourse to th' flying leap;
To a black face have sometimes ow'd escape,
And Hounslow-Heath has prov'd the worth of crape.

But how, you ask, can we e'er hope to soar
Above these scenes, and rise to tragic lore?
Too oft, alas, we've forc'd th' unwilling tear,
And petrified the heart with real fear.
Macbeth a harvest of applause will reap,
For some of us, I fear, have murder'd sleep;
His lady too with grace will sleep and talk.
Our females have been us'd at night to walk.

Sometimes, indeed, so various is our art,
An actor may improve and mend his part;
"Give me a horse," bawls Richard, like a drone,
We'll find a man would help himself to one.
Grant us your favour, put us to the test,
To gain your smiles we'll do our very best;
And, without dread of future turnkey Lockits,
Thus, in an honest way, still pick your pockets.

Published in *Annual Register, or a View of the History, Politics, and Literature for the Year 1801, Volume 43* in 1802, probably written in 1801.

I've Gotten a Rock, I've Gotten a Reel
—Susanna Blamire (1747-1794)

Air—The White Cockade

I've gotten a rock, I've gotten a reel,
I've gotten a wee bit spinning–wheel;
An' by the whirling rim I've found
How the weary, weary warl goes round.
'Tis roun' an' roun' the spokes they go,
Now ane is up, an' ane is low;
'Tis by ups and downs in Fortune's wheel,
That mony ane gets a rock to reel.

I've seen a lassie barefoot gae,
Look dash'd an' blate, wi' nought to say;
But as the wheel turn'd round again,
She chirp'd an' talk'd, nor seem'd the same:
Sae fine she goes, sae far aglee,
That folks she kenn'd she canna see;
An' fleeching chiels around her thrang,
Till she miskens her a' day lang.

There's Jock, when the bit lass was poor,
Ne'er trudg'd o'er the lang mossy moor,
Though now to the knees he wades, I trow,
Through winter's weet an' winter's snow:
An' Pate declar'd the ither morn,
She was like a lily amang the corn;
Though ance he swore her dazzling een
Were bits o' glass that black'd had been.

Now, lassies, I hae found it out,
What men make a' this phrase about;

For when they praise your blinking ee,
'Tis certain that your gowd they see:
An' when they talk o' roses bland,
They think o' the roses o' your land;
But should dame Fortune turn her wheel,
They'd aff in a dance of a threesome reel.

Published in 1842 in *The Poetical Works of Miss Susanna Blamire, "The Muse of Cumberland"*, thought to have been written around 1790.

Love and Sleep
—Algernon Charles Swinburne (1837-1909)

Lying asleep between the strokes of night
    I saw my love lean over my sad bed,
    Pale as the duskiest lily's leaf or head,
Smooth-skinned and dark, with bare throat made to
        bite,
Too wan for blushing and too warm for white,
    But perfect-coloured without white or red.
    And her lips opened amorously, and said –
I wist not what, saving one word – Delight.

And all her face was honey to my mouth,
    And all her body pasture to mine eyes;
        The long lithe arms and hotter hands than fire,
The quivering flanks, hair smelling of the south,
    The bright light feet, the splendid supple thighs
        And glittering eyelids of my soul's desire.

Published in *Laus Veneris: And Other Poems and Ballads*,
1876.

To A School-Boy At Eton. Yes and No
—Mary Savage (1718-1788)

My Dearest Boy,

Since time begun,
Since earth was earth, and sun was sun;
Since thought by words was brought to light,
And answer mild set passion right:
The hardest task assigned to man
(Deny it, lordlings, if ye can),
In two short words has been confined
(I beg you'll keep them in your mind,
For much upon their use depends,
To make us still continue friends).
I mean the use of No and Yea:
They are but simple words, you'll say,
'For surely, ma'am, 'tis long ago,
Since I first learned both Yes and No.'
I learned them too, when I was young,
But still they blunder on my tongue;
And though unlike as day to night,
'Tis ten to one I use them right;
For Yes will run, when No should drudge,
Or Yes won't stir, and No will trudge;
And sure if they'll dispute with me,
They won't (as yet) with you agree.

But that you may little guard
Against their blows, when they come hard,
We'll state a few familiar cases,
To take the mask from both their faces.

If you an apple-tree should spy,
With fruit delicious hanging high,
Secure from sight and out of bounds,
Where no preposter comes his rounds,
And chums at hands to lend a lift,
To have a taste you might make shift,
And Yes would then, with all its force,
As sure be first as headstrong horse:
But should be chance the fact be known,
Or pain in stomach cause a groan,
And make your worship cry out 'Oh!',
Then how you'll wish you had said No.

In winter's morn, if ice abound,
Or white with snow appears the ground,
Or heavy rain from clouds descend,
Or stormy winds the branches rend;
Should you submit to wicked No,
And lay in bed, whilst others go
With cautious steps and well-conned book,
To watch the Doctor's mystic look;
When next you're called, and found to fail,
You'll grieve that Yes did not prevail.

Returned to school, with cash in hand,
Full near your elbow Yes will stand:
In tempting shape of top and whip,
Or hoop to drive, or rope to skip,
Ere long as swift as lightning run
For hackney tit, or boat, or gun.
Perhaps some buck, with lively face,
More full of spirit than of grace,
With gay deportment may advance
A scheme at cards, to try your chance:
Or else advise a cheerful glass,

A few years hence, perhaps a lass,
Unmarked the cash will glide away,
And naught but empty pockets stay.
Then, if a friend distressed should come,
And ask your help—what says my son?
'A trifling Yes has ruled my day;
I naught for thee but sighs can pay.'

'Tis fit that pleasure have a share—
Always to labour, who can bear?—
But prior claims in life you'll find,
When social duties touch your mind;
And time's slow hand shall point the way,
Where to object, and when to obey:
A task too hard for me to teach;
Should I proceed, you'd say I preach.

 few words more, and I am off:
At prudence fools will often scoff;
If you a parent's look attend,
Or fear in play to hurt a friend,
And won't your only farthing lend,
You'll be the jest of every wight,
Whose passions are his rule of right.
But let the laugh go ever so,
Be virtue's friend, and vice's foe,
And never blush at proper No.

Published in 1777 in *Poems on Various Subjects and Occasions*.

151

On Marriage
—Richard Crashaw (1613-1649)

I would be married, but I'd have no wife;
I would be married to a single life.

Published in *Steps to the Temple. Sacred Poems, With The Delights of the Muses*, 1648.

The Moon-Flower
—Lala Fisher (1872-1929)

I know a valley. Through its solitude
A brown road winds towards a mountain crest;
There gnarly ti-trees dripping sweetness rest,
And grasses bend, too heavily bedewed.

In that still valley by the still lagoon,
A ruined homestead for her secret shrine,
Dwells Beauty's self, half-earthly, half-divine—
Thrilling, I saw her waken to the Moon.

In peaks of emerald the cactus crept,
And there o'er rafters falling to decay,
A miracle of flowers, spray on spray,
Burst into perfect life while Nature slept.

First a slim silver riband from the sky
Uncurled green fronds from each imprisoned bud,
Then, one by one, bathed in the beaming flood,
Like ghost-notes in a spirit litany.

They blossomed out before my very eyes,
Great chalices of snow filled up with light,
Set in the dusky splendour of the night
They seemed a vision from immortal skies.

Hidden in shadow near the still lagoon
Nightly I worship at a secret shrine,
There on a ruin—lily-white, divine,
Is Beauty lying naked to the Moon!

Published in *Grass Flowering: Verses*, 1915, but first appeared in *Lilley's Magazine* in 1911.

De Bell of St Michel
—William Henry Drummond (1854-1907)

Go 'way, go 'way, don't ring no more, ole bell of Saint
    Michel,
For if you do, I can't stay here, you know dat very
    well,
No matter how I close ma ear, I can't shut out de
    soun',
It rise so high 'bove all de noise of dis beeg Yankee
    town.
An' w'en it ring, I t'ink I feel de cool, cool summer
    breeze
Dat's blow across Lac Peezagonk, an' play among de
    trees,
Dey're makin' hay, I know mese'f, can smell de
    pleasant smell
O! how I wish I could be dere to-day on Saint Michel!

It's fonny t'ing, for me I'm sure, dat's travel
    ev'ryw'ere,
How moche I t'ink of long ago w'en I be leevin' dere;
I can't 'splain dat at all, at all, mebbe it's naturel,
But I can't help it w'en I hear de bell of Saint Michel.

Dere's plaintee t'ing I don't forget, but I remember
    bes'
De spot I fin' wan day on June de small san'piper's
    nes'
An' dat hole on de reever w'ere I ketch de beeg, beeg
    trout
Was very nearly pull me in before I pull heem out.

An' leetle Elodie Leclaire, I wonner if she still
Leev jus' sam' place she use to leev on 'noder side de
    hill,

But s'pose she marry Joe Barbeau, dat's alway hangin'
    roun'
Since I am lef' ole Saint Michel for work on Yankee
    town.

Ah! dere she go, ding dong, ding dong, its back,
    encore again
An' ole chanson come on ma head of "a la claire
    fontaine,"
I'm not surprise it soun' so sweet, more sweeter I can
    tell
For wit' de song also I hear de bell of Saint Michel.

It's very strange about dat bell, go ding dong all de
    w'ile
For when I'm small garçon at school, can't hear it half
    a mile;
But seems more farder I get off from Church of Saint
    Michel,
De more I see de ole village an' louder soun' de bell.

O! all de monee dat I mak' w'en I be travel roun'
Can't kip me long away from home on dis beeg
    Yankee town,
I t'ink I'll settle down again on Parish Saint Michel,
An' leev an' die more satisfy so long I hear dat bell.

Published in 1897 in *The Habitant, and Other French-Canadian Poems.*

To My Dear and Loving Husband
—Anne Bradstreet (c1612-1672)

If ever two were one, then surely we.
If ever man were loved by wife, then thee;
If ever wife was happy in a man,
Compare with me, ye woman, if you can.
I prize thy love more than whole mines of gold,
Or all the riches that the east doth hold.
My love is such that rivers cannot quench,
Nor aught but love from thee, give recompense.
Thy love is such I can no way repay,
The heavens reward thee manifold, I pray.
Then while we live, in love let's so persevere
That when we live no more, we may live ever.

Probably written between 1641 and 1643 but not published until 1678 in *Several Poems Compiled with Great Variety of Wit and Learning, Full of Delight.*

A Letter from a Girl to Her Own Old Age
—Alice Meynell (1847-1922)

Lete vedrai—DANTE.

Listen, and when thy hand this paper presses,
O time-worn woman, think of her who blesses
What thy thin fingers touch, with her caresses.

O mother, for the weight of years that break thee!
O daughter, for slow time must yet awake thee,
And from the changes of my heart must make thee!

O fainting traveller, morn is gray in heaven.
Dost thou remember how the clouds were driven?
And are they calm about the fall of even?

Pause near the ending of thy long migration;
For this one sudden hour of desolation
Appeals to one hour of thy meditation.

Suffer, O silent one, that I remind thee
Of the great hills that stormed the sky behind thee,
Of the wild winds of power that have resigned thee.

Know that the mournful plain where thou must
    wander
Is but a gray and silent world, but ponder
The misty mountains of the morning yonder.

Listen:-the mountain winds with rain were fretting,
And sudden gleams the mountain-tops besetting.
I cannot let thee fade to death, forgetting.

What part of this wild heart of mine I know not
Will follow with thee where the great winds blow not,
And where the young flowers of the mountain grow
    not.

Yet let my letter with thy lost thoughts in it
Tell what the way was when thou didst begin it,
And win with thee the goal when thou shalt win it.

I have not writ this letter of divining
To make a glory of thy silent pining,
A triumph of thy mute and strange declining.

Only one youth, and the bright life was shrouded;
Only one morning, and the day was clouded;
And one old age with all regrets is crowded.

O hush, O hush! Thy tears my words are steeping.
O hush, hush, hush! So full, the fount of weeping?
Poor eyes, so quickly moved, so near to sleeping?

Pardon the girl; such strange desires beset her.
Poor woman, lay aside the mournful letter
That breaks thy heart; the one who wrote, forget her:

The one who now thy faded features guesses,
With filial fingers thy gray hair caresses,
With morning tears thy mournful twilight blesses.

Published in *Preludes*, 1875.

Call for the Robin Redbreast and the Wren
—John Webster (c1580-c1634)

Call for the robin redbreast, and the wren,
Since o'er shady groves they hover,
And with leaves and flowers do cover
The friendless bodies of unburied men.
Call unto his funeral dole
The ant, the fieldmouse, and the mole,
To rear him hillocks that shall keep him warm,
And (when gay tombs are robb'd) sustain no harm;
But keep the wolf far thence, that 's foe to men,
For with his nails he 'll dig them up again.
They would not bury him 'cause he died in a quarrel;
But I have an answer for them:
Let holy Church receive him duly,
Since he paid the church-tithes truly.
His wealth is summ'd, and this is all his store,
This poor men get, and great men get no more.
Now the wares are gone, we may shut up shop.
Bless you all, good people.

Said by 'Cornelia' in the play, *The White Devil*, first
performed in 1612.

When Stretch'd On One's Bed
—Jane Austen (1775-1817)

When stretch'd on one's bed
With a fierce-throbbing head,
Which precludes alike thought or repose,
How little one cares
For the grandest affairs
That may busy the world as it goes!

How little one feels
For the waltzes and reels
Of our Dance-loving friends at a Ball!
How slight one's concern
To conjecture or learn
What their flounces or hearts may befall.

How little one minds
If a company dines
On the best that the Season affords!
How short is one's muse
O'er the Sauces and Stews,
Or the Guests, be they Beggars or Lords.

How little the Bells,
Ring they Peels, toll they Knells,
Can attract our attention or Ears!
The Bride may be married,
The Corse may be carried
And touch nor our hopes nor our fears.

Our own bodily pains
Ev'ry faculty chains;
We can feel on no subject besides.

Tis in health and in ease
We the power must seize
For our friends and our souls to provide.

Octr 27. 1811

Written in 1811 three days before her first published novel,
Sense and Sensibility.

Verse for a Certain Dog
—Dorothy Parker (1893-1967)

Such glorious faith as fills your limpid eyes,
Dear little friend of mine, I never knew.
All-innocent are you, and yet all-wise.
(For Heaven's sake, stop worrying that shoe!)
You look about, and all you see is fair;
This mighty globe was made for you alone.
Of all the thunderous ages, you're the heir.
(Get off the pillow with that dirty bone!)

A skeptic world you face with steady gaze;
High in young pride you hold your noble head,
Gayly you meet the rush of roaring days.
(Must you eat puppy biscuit on the bed?)
Lancelike your courage, gleaming swift and strong,
Yours the white rapture of a winged soul,
Yours is a spirit like a Mayday song.
(God help you, if you break the goldfish bowl!)

'Whatever is, is good'—your gracious creed.
You wear your joy of living like a crown.
Love lights your simplest act, your every deed

(Drop it, I tell you- put that kitten down!)
You are God's kindliest gift of all—a friend.
Your shining loyalty unflecked by doubt,
You ask but leave to follow to the end.
(Couldn't you wait until I took you out?)

First published in 1924.

Song: Hidden Flame
—John Dryden (1631-1700)

I feed a flame within, which so torments me
That it both pains my heart, and yet contains me:
'Tis such a pleasing smart, and I so love it,
That I had rather die than once remove it.

Yet he, for whom I grieve, shall never know it;
My tongue does not betray, nor my eyes show it.
Not a sigh, nor a tear, my pain discloses,
But they fall silently, like dew on roses.

Thus, to prevent my Love from being cruel,
My heart's the sacrifice, as 'tis the fuel;
And while I suffer this to give him quiet,
My faith rewards my love, though he deny it.

On his eyes will I gaze, and there delight me;
While I conceal my love no frown can fright me.
To be more happy I dare not aspire,
Nor can I fall more low, mounting no higher.

Sung by 'Asteria' in *Secret-Love, Or the Maiden-Queen*, first
performed in 1667.

The Blessed Damozel
—Dante Gabriel Rossetti (1828-1882)

The blessed damozel lean'd out
    From the gold bar of Heaven;
Her eyes were deeper than the depth
    Of waters still'd at even;
She had three lilies in her hand,
    And the stars in her hair were seven.

Her robe, ungirt from clasp to hem,
    No wrought flowers did adorn,
But a white rose of Mary's gift,
    For service meetly worn;
Her hair that lay along her back
    Was yellow like ripe corn.

Her seem'd she scarce had been a day
    One of God's choristers;
The wonder was not yet quite gone
    From that still look of hers;
Albeit, to them she left, her day
    Had counted as ten years.

(To one, it is ten years of years.
    . . . Yet now, and in this place,
Surely she lean'd o'er me—her hair
    Fell all about my face. . . .
Nothing: the autumn-fall of leaves.
    The whole year sets apace.)

It was the rampart of God's house
    That she was standing on;
By God built over the sheer depth

The which is Space begun;
So high, that looking downward thence
She scarce could see the sun.

It lies in Heaven, across the flood
Of ether, as a bridge.
Beneath, the tides of day and night
With flame and darkness ridge
The void, as low as where this earth
Spins like a fretful midge.

Around her, lovers, newly met
'Mid deathless love's acclaims,
Spoke evermore among themselves
Their heart-remembered names;
And the souls mounting up to God
Went by her like thin flames.

And still she bow'd herself and stoop'd
Out of the circling charm;
Until her bosom must have made
The bar she lean'd on warm,
And the lilies lay as if asleep
Along her bended arm.

From the fix'd place of Heaven she saw
Time like a pulse shake fierce
Through all the worlds. Her gaze still strove
Within the gulf to pierce
Its path; and now she spoke as when
The stars sang in their spheres.

The sun was gone now; the curl'd moon
Was like a little feather
Fluttering far down the gulf; and now

She spoke through the still weather.
Her voice was like the voice of the stars
Had when they sang together.

(Ah sweet! Even now, in that bird's song,
Strove not her accents there,
Fain to be hearken'd? When those bells
Possessed the mid-day air,
Strove not her steps to reach my side
Down all the echoing stair?)

'I wish that he were come to me,
For he will come,' she said.
'Have I not pray'd in Heaven?—on earth,
Lord, Lord, has he not pray'd?
Are not two prayers a perfect strength?
And shall I feel afraid?

'When round his head the aureole clings,
And he is cloth'd in white,
I'll take his hand and go with him
To the deep wells of light;
As unto a stream we will step down,
And bathe there in God's sight.

'We two will stand beside that shrine,
Occult, withheld, untrod,
Whose lamps are stirr'd continually
With prayer sent up to God;
And see our old prayers, granted, melt
Each like a little cloud.

'We two will lie i' the shadow of
That living mystic tree
Within whose secret growth the Dove

Is sometimes felt to be,
While every leaf that His plumes touch
Saith His Name audibly.

'And I myself will teach to him,
I myself, lying so,
The songs I sing here; which his voice
Shall pause in, hush'd and slow,
And find some knowledge at each pause,
Or some new thing to know.'

(Alas! We two, we two, thou say'st!
Yea, one wast thou with me
That once of old. But shall God lift
To endless unity
The soul whose likeness with thy soul
Was but its love for thee?)

'We two,' she said, 'will seek the groves
Where the lady Mary is,
With her five handmaidens, whose names
Are five sweet symphonies,
Cecily, Gertrude, Magdalen,
Margaret and Rosalys.

'Circlewise sit they, with bound locks
And foreheads garlanded;
Into the fine cloth white like flame
Weaving the golden thread,
To fashion the birth-robes for them
Who are just born, being dead.

'He shall fear, haply, and be dumb:
Then will I lay my cheek
To his, and tell about our love,

Not once abash'd or weak:
And the dear Mother will approve
My pride, and let me speak.

'Herself shall bring us, hand in hand,
    To Him round whom all souls
Kneel, the clear-ranged unnumber'd heads
    Bowed with their aureoles:
And angels meeting us shall sing
    To their citherns and citoles.

'There will I ask of Christ the Lord
    Thus much for him and me:—
Only to live as once on earth
    With Love,—only to be,
As then awhile, for ever now
    Together, I and he.'

She gaz'd and listen'd and then said,
    Less sad of speech than mild,—
'All this is when he comes.' She ceas'd.
    The light thrill'd towards her, fill'd
With angels in strong level flight.
    Her eyes prayed, and she smil'd.

(I saw her smile.) But soon their path
    Was vague in distant spheres:
And then she cast her arms along
    The golden barriers,
And laid her face between her hands,
    And wept. (I heard her tears.)

First published in1850 in the magazine, *The Germ,* and
revised and republished in 1856, 1870 and 1873.

Woman's Hard Fate
—A Lady

How wretched is a woman's fate,
　No happy change her fortune knows;
Subject to man in every state,
　How can she then be free from woes?

In youth, a father's stern command
　And jealous eyes control her will;
A lordly brother watchful stands
　To keep her closer captive still.

The tyrant husband next appears,
　With awful and contracted brow;
No more a lover's form he wears:
　Her slaves become her sovereign now.

If from this fatal bondage free,
　And not by marriage-chains confined,
But, blessed with single life, can see
　A parent fond, a brother kind;

Yet love usurps her tender breast,
　And paints a phoenix to her eyes:
Some darling youth disturbs her rest,
　And painful sighs in secret rise.

Oh cruel powers, since you've designed
　That man, vain man, should bear the sway,
To a slave's fetters add a slavish mind,
　That I may cheerfully your will obey.

Published in *The Gentleman's Magazine*, Volume 3, 1733.

Verses Inviting Stella to Tea on the Public Fast-Day [During the American War], February, MDCCLXXXI
—Anna Seward (1742-1809)

Dear Stella, midst the pious sorrow
Our Monarch bids us feel tomorrow,
The ah's! and oh's! supremely trist,
The abstinence from beef and whist,
Wisely ordained to please the Lord,
And force him whet our edgeless sword,
Till, skipping o'er th' Atlantic rill,
We cut provincial throats at will;
Midst all the penitence we feel
For merry sins—midst all the zeal
For vengeance on the saucy foe,
Who lays our boasted legions low,
I wish, when sullen evening comes,
To gild for me its falling glooms,
You would, without cold pause, agree
Beneath these walls to sip your tea.
From the chaste, fragrant Indian weed
Our sins no pampering juices feed;
And though the Hours, with contrite faces,
May banish the ungodly aces,
And take of food a sparing bit,
They'll gluttonise on Stella's wit.

'Tea,' cries a Patriot, 'on that day!
'Twere good you flung the drug away!
Remembering 'twas the cruel source
Of sad distrust, and long divorce,
'Twixt nations which, combined, had hurled
Their conquering javelin round the world.

'O Indian shrub! Thy fragrant flowers
To England's weal had deadly powers,
When Tyranny, with impious hand,
To venom turned its essence bland;
To venom subtle, fierce and fell,
As drenched the dart of Isdabel.

'Have we forgot that cursed libation,
That cost the lives of half the nation?
When Boston, with indignant thought,
Saw poison in the perfumed draught,
And caused her troubled Bay to be
But one vast bowl of bitter tea;
While Até, chiefly-bidden guest,
Came sternly to the fatal feast,
And mingled with th' envenomed flood
Brothers', parents' children's blood:
Dire as the banquet Atreus served,
When his own sons Thyestes carved,
And Phoebus, shrinking from the sight,
Drew o'er his orb the pall of night.

'Tomorrow then, at least, refrain,
Nor quaff thy gasping country's bane!
For, O! reflect, poetic daughter,
'Twas vanquished Britain's laurel-water!'

Appeared in *Verses and Prose, 1781 Feb-1782 August*;
written in 1781.

To A Child of Quality of Five Years Old
—Matthew Prior (1664-1721)

The Author suppos'd Forty.

Lords, knights, and squires, the numerous band
  That wear the fair Miss Mary's fetters,
Were summoned by her high command
  To show their passions by their letters.

My pen amongst the rest I took,
  Lest those bright eyes, that cannot read,
Should dart their kindling fire, and look
  The power they have to be obey'd.

Nor quality, nor reputation,
  Forbid me yet my flame to tell;
Dear Five-years-old befriends my passion,
  And I may write till she can spell.

For, while she makes her silkworms beds
  With all the tender things I swear;
Whilst all the house my passion reads,
  In papers round her baby's hair;

She may receive and own my flame;
  For, though the strictest prudes should know it,
She'll pass for a most virtuous dame,
  And I for an unhappy poet.

Then too, alas! when she shall tear
  The rhymes some younger rival sends,
She'll give me leave to write, I fear,
  And we shall still continue friends.

For, as our different ages move,
 'Tis so ordain'd (would Fate but mend it!),
That I shall be past making love
 When she begins to comprehend it.

Published in 1704 in Tonson's *Poetical Miscellanies: the
fifth part* but written four years earlier in 1700 when the
poet was 36 years old.

Kubla Khan: Or, A Vision in a Dream: A Fragment
—Samuel Taylor Coleridge (1772-1834)

In Xanadu did Kubla Khan
 A stately pleasure-dome decree:
Where Alph, the sacred river, ran
Through caverns measureless to man
 Down to a sunless sea.

So twice five miles of fertile ground
With walls and towers were girdled round:
And there were gardens bright with sinuous rills,
Where blossomed many an incense-bearing tree;
And here were forests ancient as the hills,
Enfolding sunny spots of greenery.

But oh! that deep romantic chasm which slanted
Down the green hill athwart a cedarn cover!
A savage place! as holy and enchanted
As e'er beneath a waning moon was haunted
By woman wailing for her demon-lover!
And from this chasm, with ceaseless turmoil seething,
As if this earth in fast thick pants were breathing,
A mighty fountain momently was forced:
Amid whose swift half-intermitted burst
Huge fragments vaulted like rebounding hail,
Or chaffy grain beneath the thresher's flail:
And 'mid these dancing rocks at once and ever
It flung up momently the sacred river.
Five miles meandering with a mazy motion
Through wood and dale the sacred river ran,
Then reached the caverns measureless to man,
And sank in tumult to a lifeless ocean:

And 'mid this tumult Kubla heard from far
Ancestral voices prophesying war!

The shadow of the dome of pleasure
Floated midway on the waves;
Where was heard the mingled measure
From the fountain and the caves.
It was a miracle of rare device,
A sunny pleasure-dome with caves of ice!

A damsel with a dulcimer
In a vision once I saw:
It was an Abyssinian maid,
And on her dulcimer she played,
Singing of Mount Abora.
Could I revive within me
Her symphony and song,
To such a deep delight 'twould win me
That with music loud and long
I would build that dome in air,
That sunny dome! those caves of ice!
And all who heard should see them there,
And all should cry, Beware! Beware!
His flashing eyes, his floating hair!
Weave a circle round him thrice,
And close your eyes with holy dread,
For he on honey-dew hath fed
And drunk the milk of Paradise.

Written in 1797 but not published until 1816 in
Christabel: Kubla Khan : a Vision ; The Pains of Sleep.

Index of Poets

Index of Titles

Index of First Lines

185